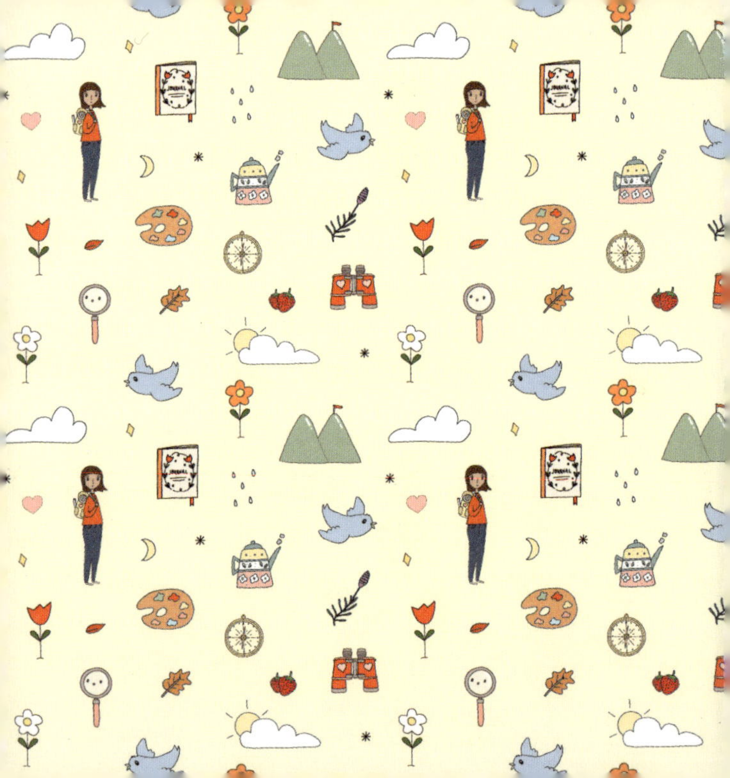

HAPPIFUL

100 uplifting illustrations for your journey to JOY!

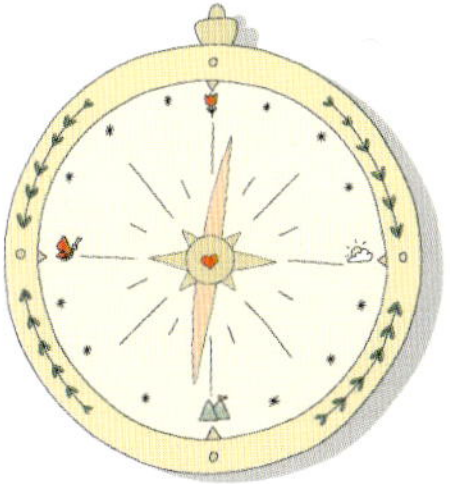

BY JANA RUSHFORTH

Published by Familius LLC, www.familius.com
PO Box 1249, Reedley, CA 93654

Familius books are available at special discounts for bulk purchases, whether for sales promotions or for family or corporate use. For more information, contact Familius Sales at orders@familius.com.

Library of Congress Control Number: 2021946068

Print ISBN 9781641706605

Printed in China

Edited by Laurie Duersch
Cover design by Jana Rushforth
Book design by Jana Rushforth

10 9 8 7 6 5 4 3 2 1

First Edition

For Harry

– You inspired every page of this book.

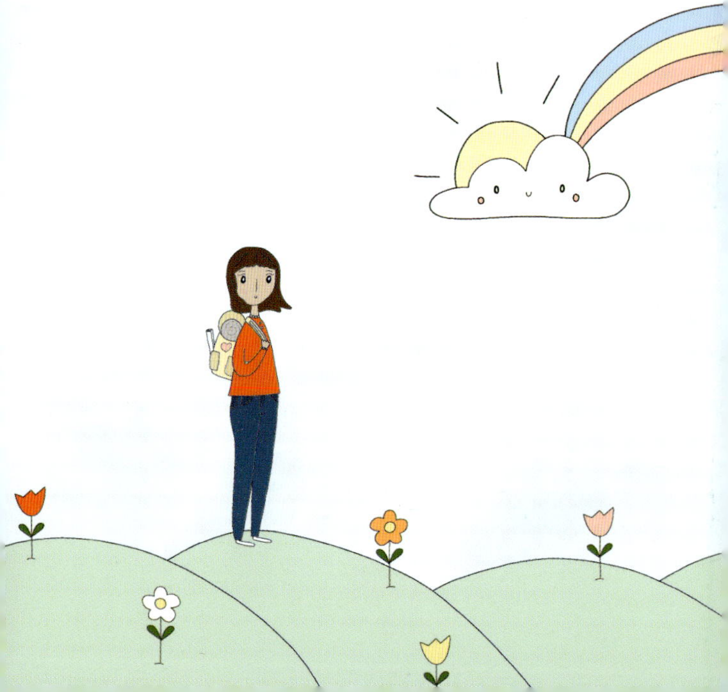

WELCOME

This little book is about following your curiosity, looking for wonder, filling your cup, & knowing you are not alone on your journey to joy.

On your explorations, this book can be your companion. So pop it in your bag or on your bedside table to refer to when you need inspiration & mindful reminders along the way.

You may like to read it from cover to cover, or turn to a random page for a daily affirmation. You can choose the path that feels right for you.

There are signposts throughout to point you towards self-care, mindfulness, & gratitude. You'll also find spots to take a rest, reflect, & enjoy the view.

Wherever you are on your quest, I hope my words & illustrations will guide you every step of the way.

So grab your backpack, set your inner compass, & focus your wonder binoculars. Let's go!

Jana xx

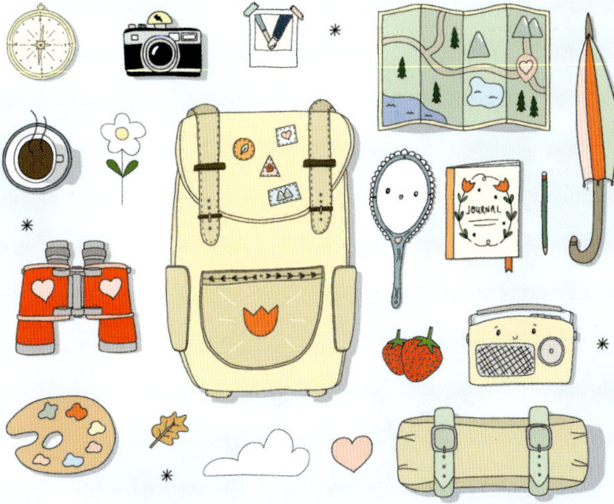
JOURNAL

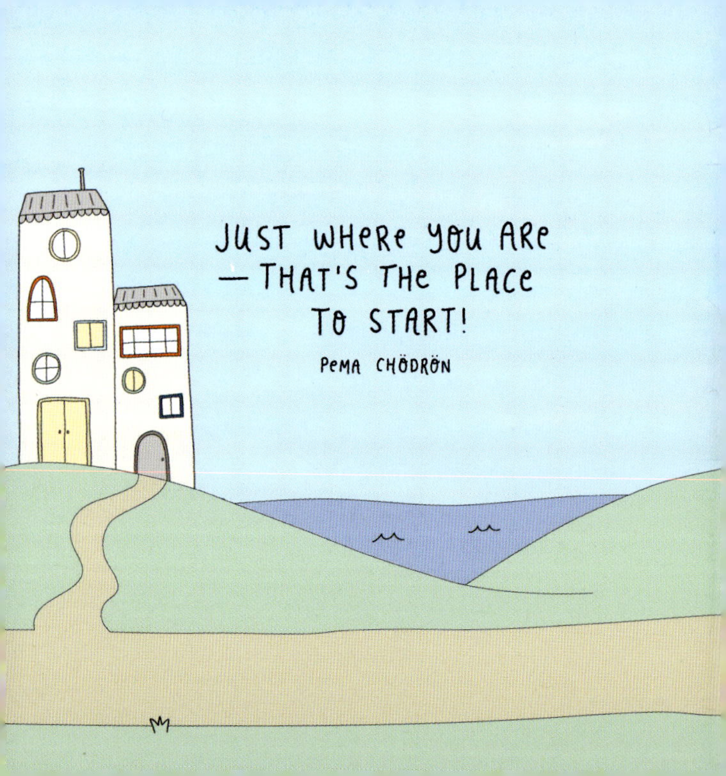
JUST WHERE YOU ARE
— THAT'S THE PLACE
TO START!
PEMA CHÖDRÖN

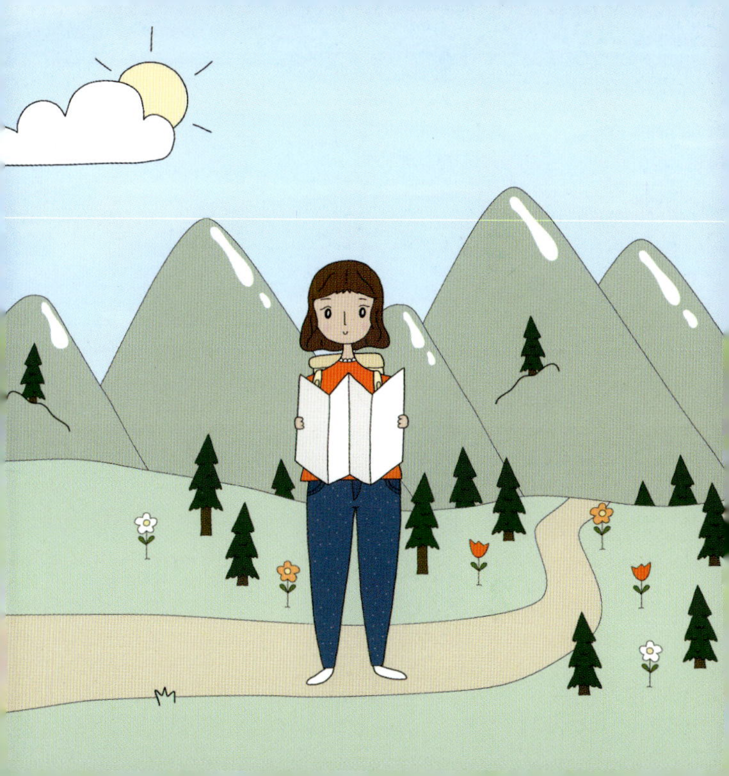

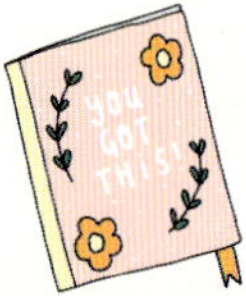

A lovely planner.

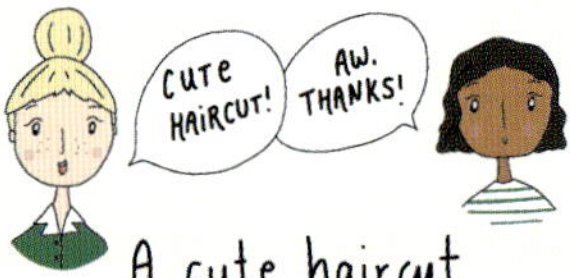

A cute haircut.

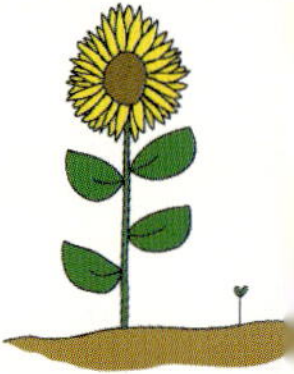

A new seas
of life or
the calend

FRESH STARTS

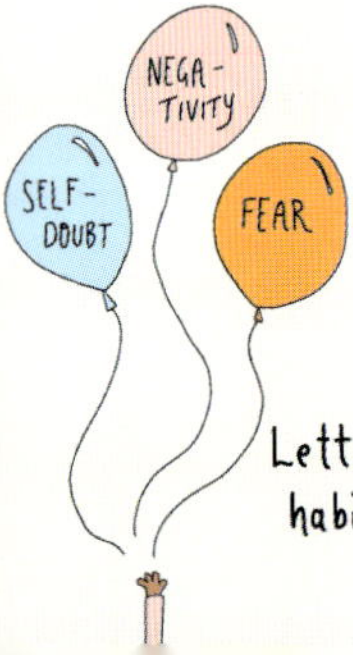

Letting go of old habits & mindsets.

A hug.

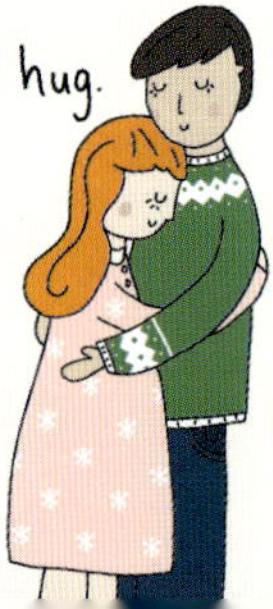

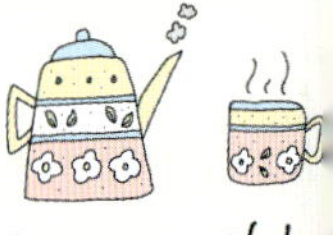

A nice cup of te

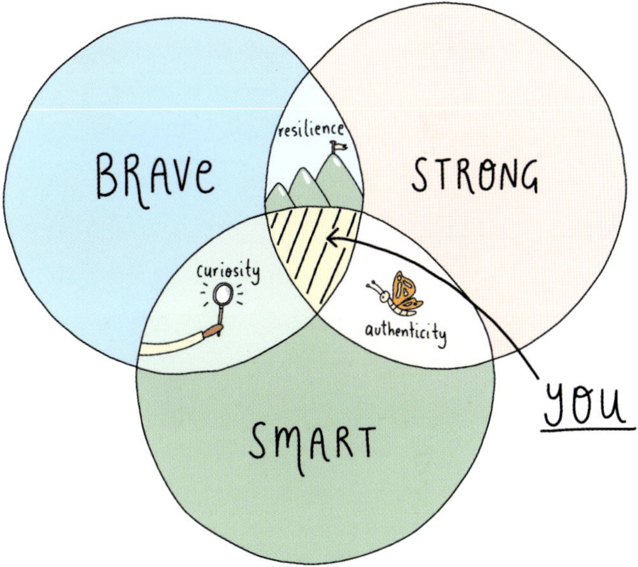
BRAVE
STRONG
resilience
curiosity
authenticity
SMART
YOU

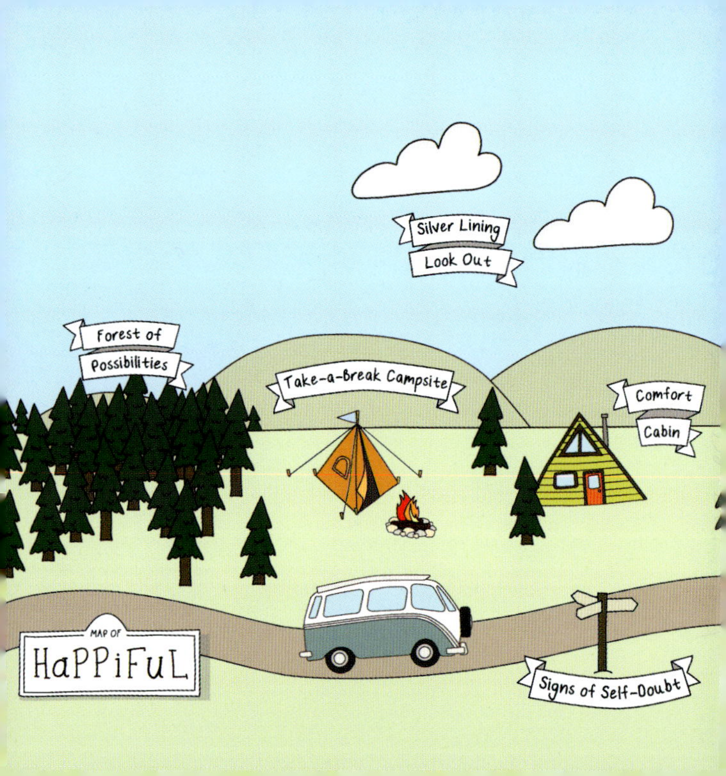
Silver Lining
Look Out
Forest of
Possibilities
Take-a-Break Campsite
Comfort
Cabin
MAP OF
HaPPiFuL
Signs of Self-Doubt

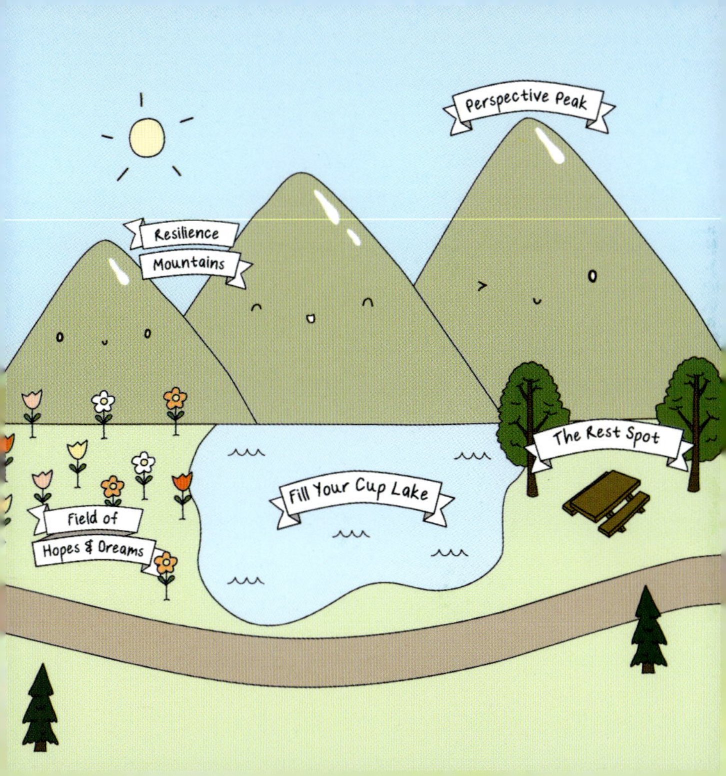
Perspective Peak
Resilience Mountains
Fill Your Cup Lake
The Rest Spot
Field of Hopes & Dreams

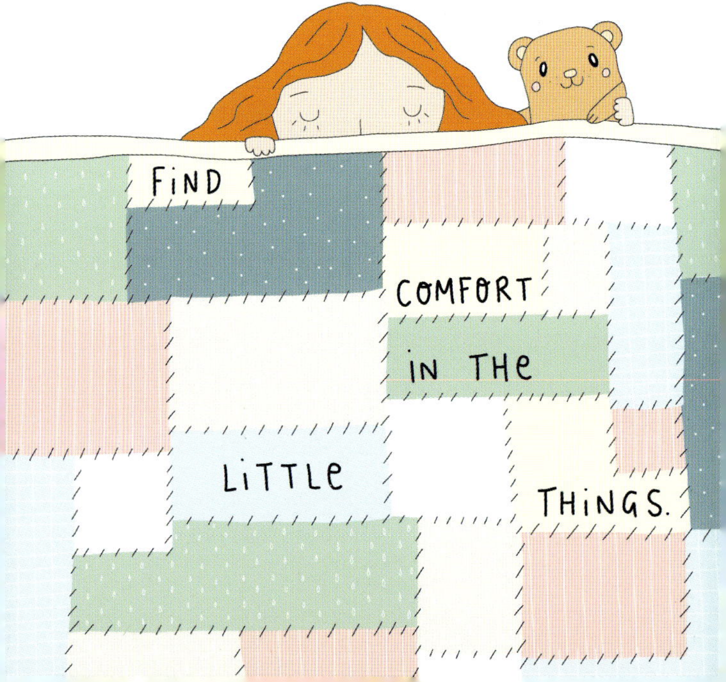
FIND
COMFORT
IN THE
LITTLE
THINGS.

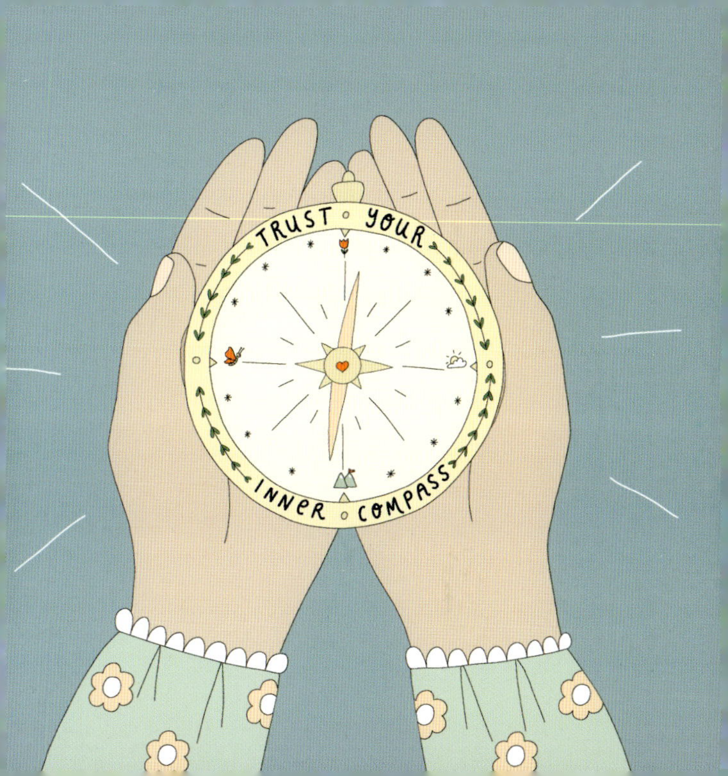
TRUST YOUR
INNER COMPASS

Visualize yourself putting on "joy seeker" sunglasses, which are heart-shaped, of course! Use these glasses to train your mind to look for moments of joy in your day.

What joy did you spot?

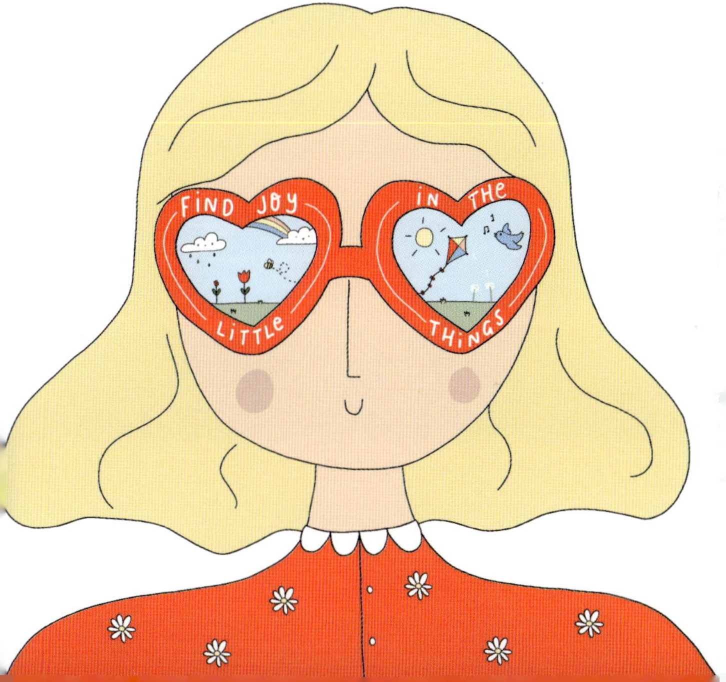
FIND JOY
LITTLE
IN THE
THINGS

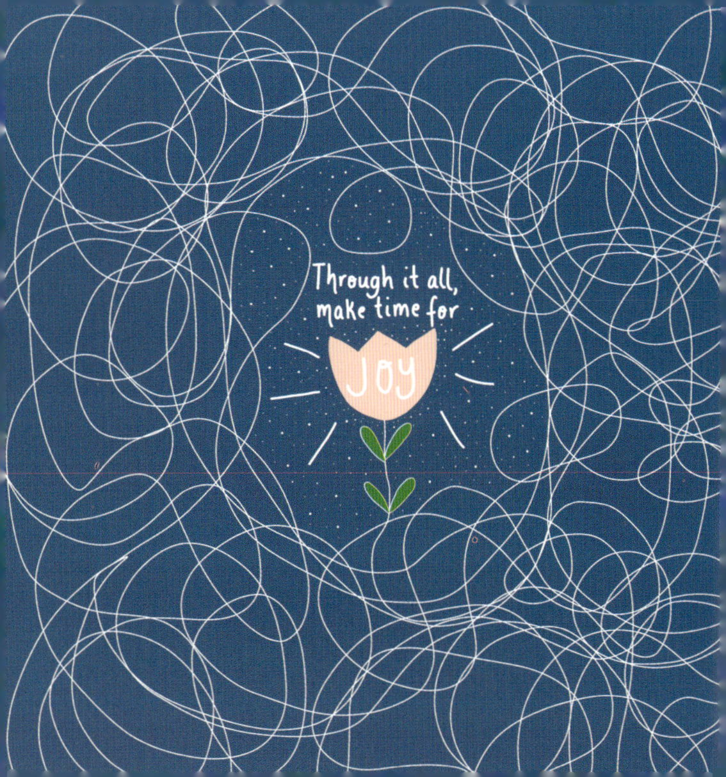
Through it all,
make time for
JOY

WAYS TO SAY "I LOVE YOU" TO YOU

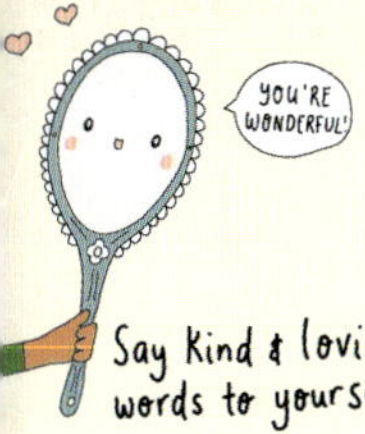

Say kind & loving words to yourself.

Pick flowers.

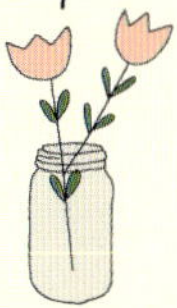

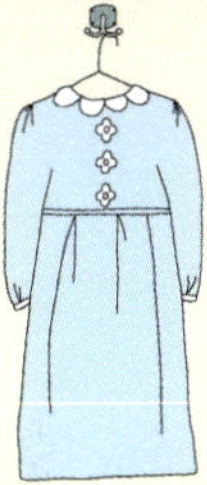

Wear the "only for special occasions" dress.

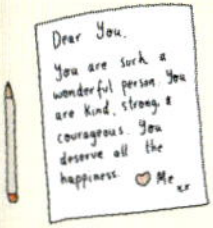

Write a love letter to you.

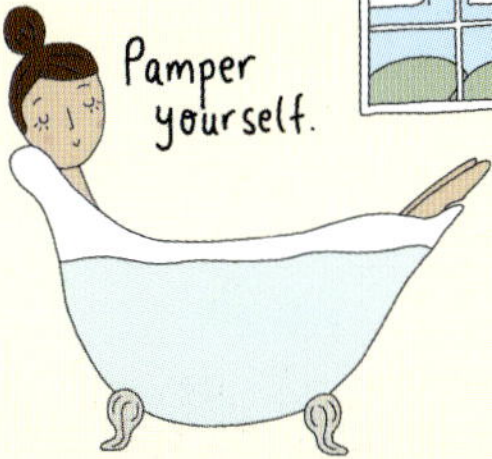

Pamper yourself.

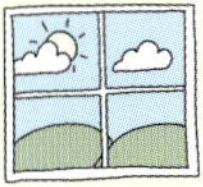

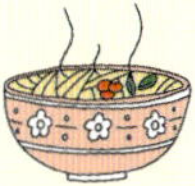

Make your favorite meal.

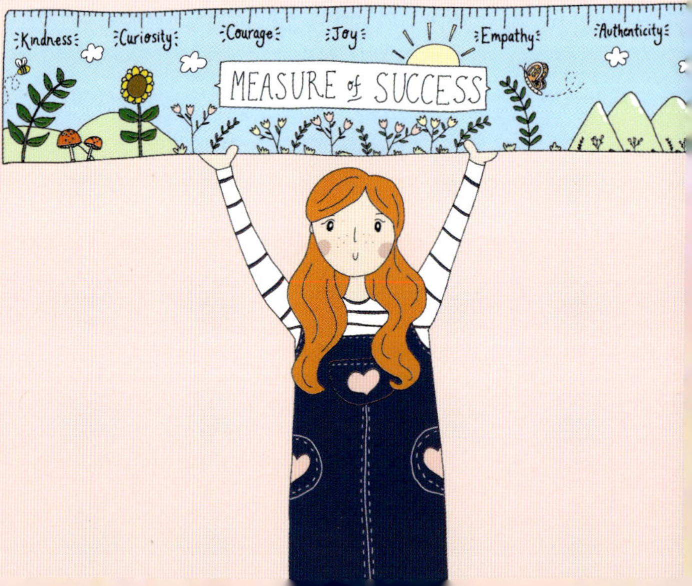
Kindness
Curiosity
Courage
Joy
Empathy
Authenticity
MEASURE of SUCCESS

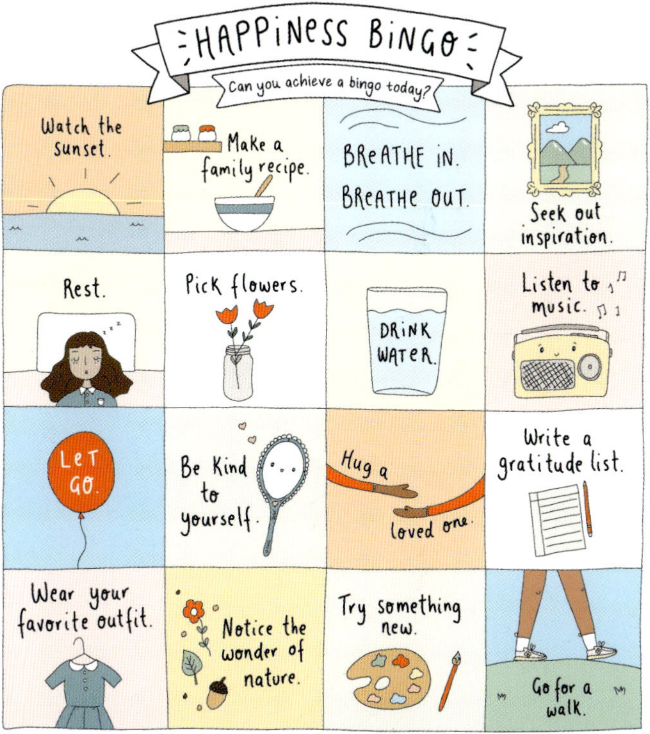
HAPPINESS BINGO
Can you achieve a bingo today?
Watch the sunset.
Make a family recipe.
BREATHE IN. BREATHE OUT.
Seek out inspiration.
Rest.
Pick flowers.
DRINK WATER.
Listen to music.
LET GO.
Be Kind to yourself.
Hug a loved one.
Write a gratitude list.
Wear your favorite outfit.
Notice the wonder of nature.
Try something new.
Go for a walk.

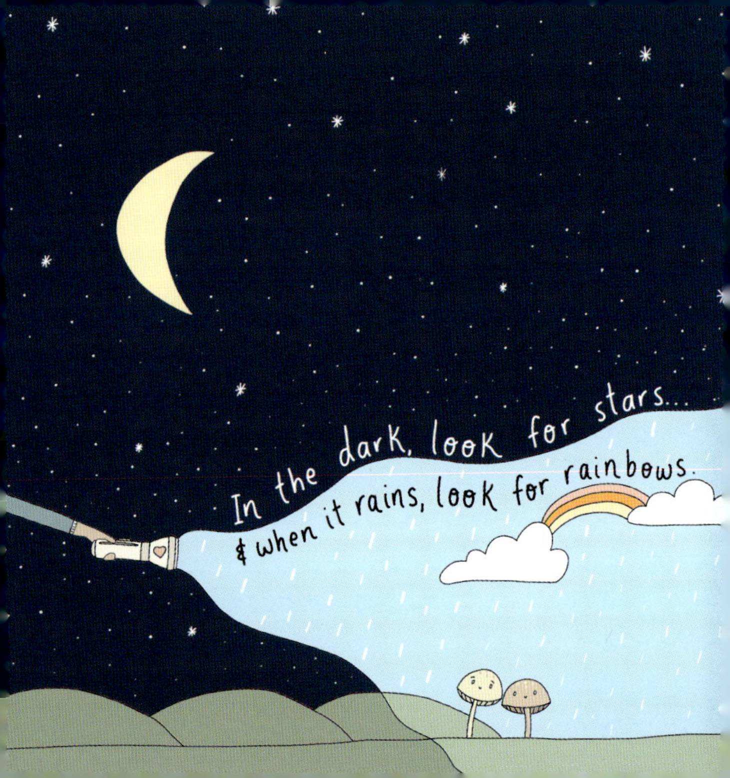
In the dark, look for stars...
& when it rains, look for rainbows.

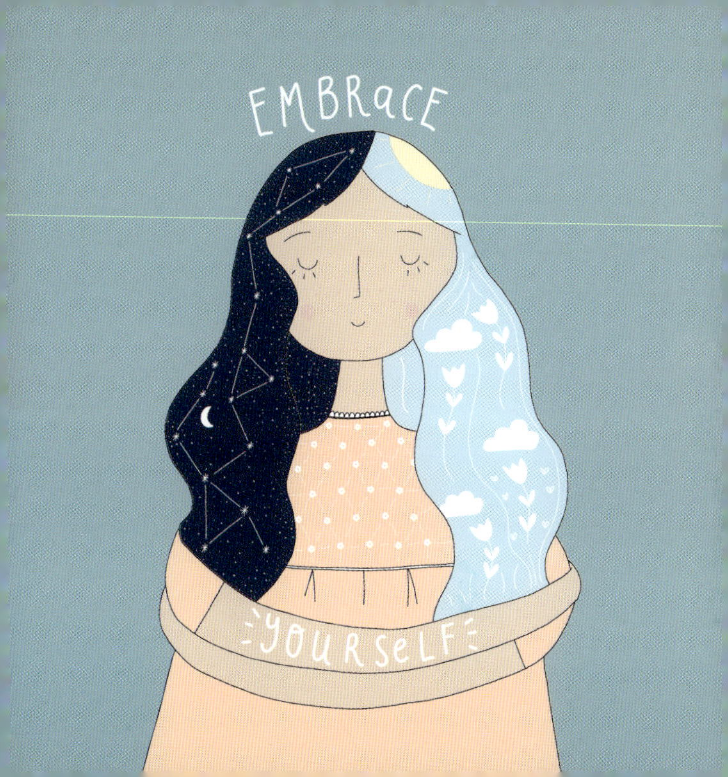
EMBRACE
YOURSELF

GROWING YOUR

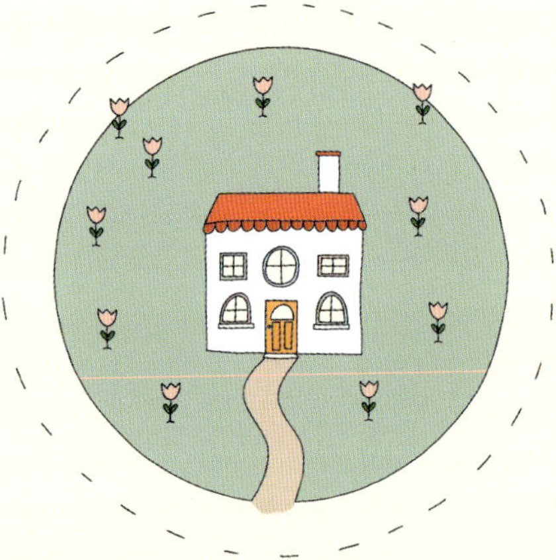

Start sowing seeds just outside your comfort zone. It may feel scary & a little bit uncomfortable at first...

COMFORT ZONE

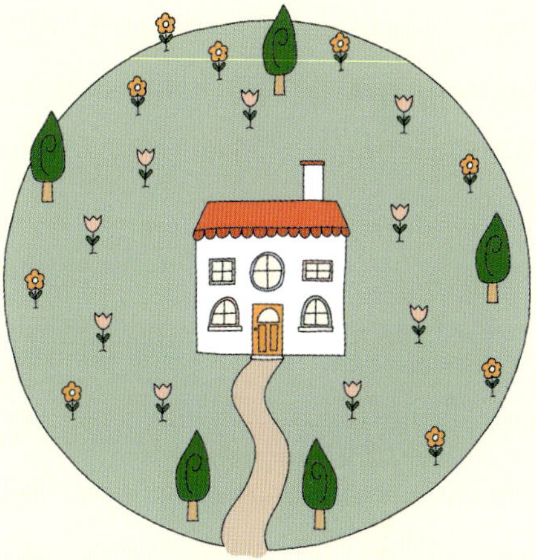

but as the seeds grow, you'll grow too, & your comfort zone will slowly expand.

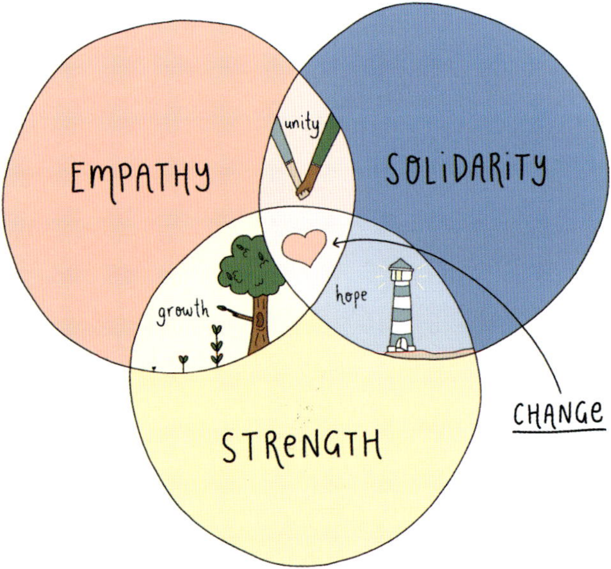
EMPATHY
SOLIDARITY
STRENGTH
unity
growth
hope
CHANGE

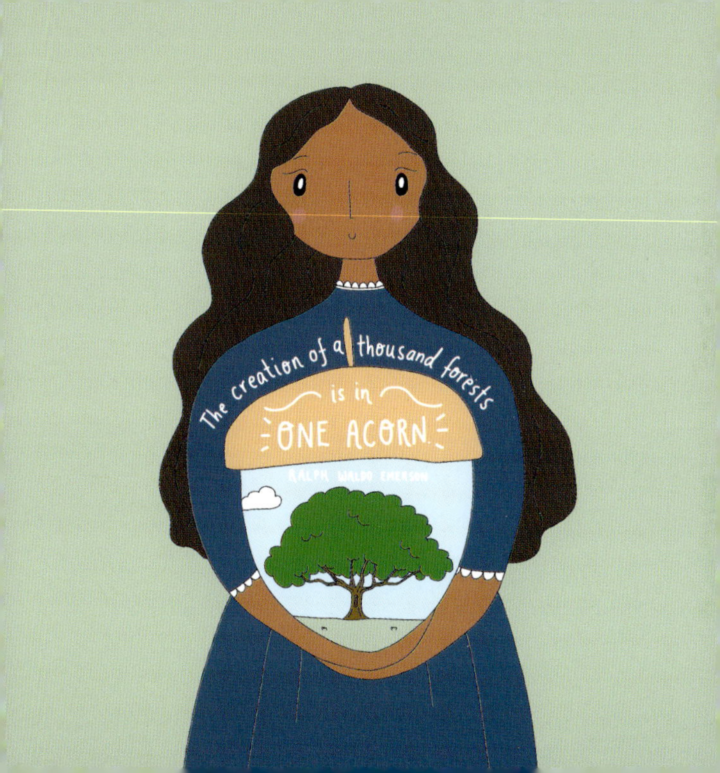
The creation of a thousand forests
is in
ONE ACORN
RALPH WALDO EMERSON

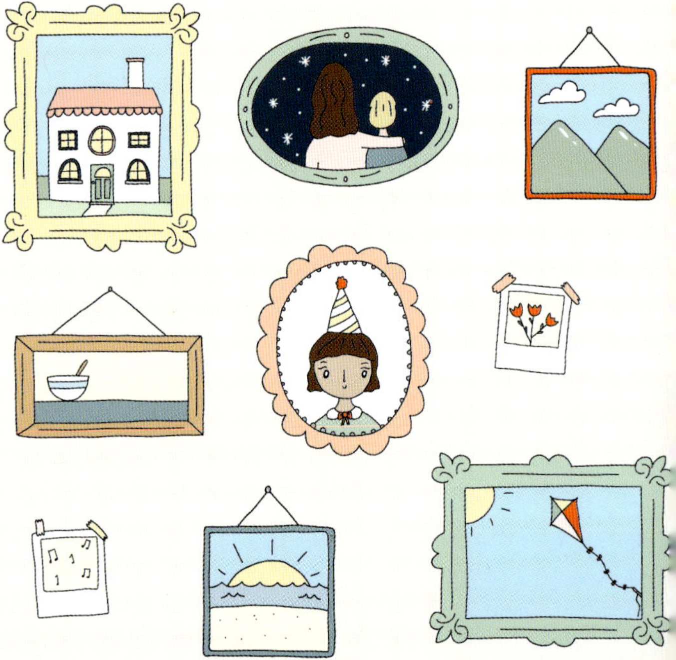

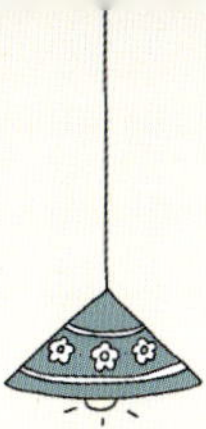

Whenever you want to capture a moment, look at it until you have a clear picture, then blink your eyes like a shutter on a camera. Frame the memory & hang it in your mind.

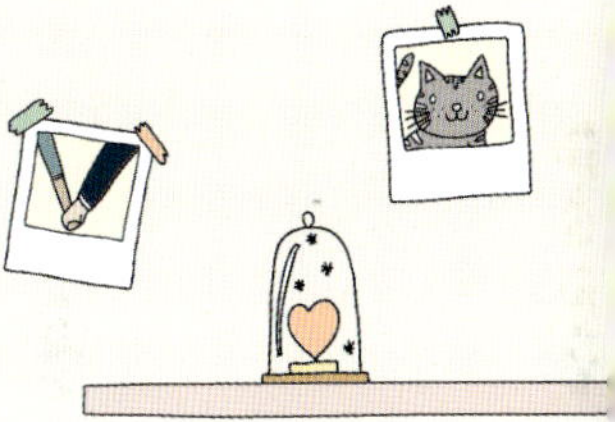

NEW BEGINNINGS

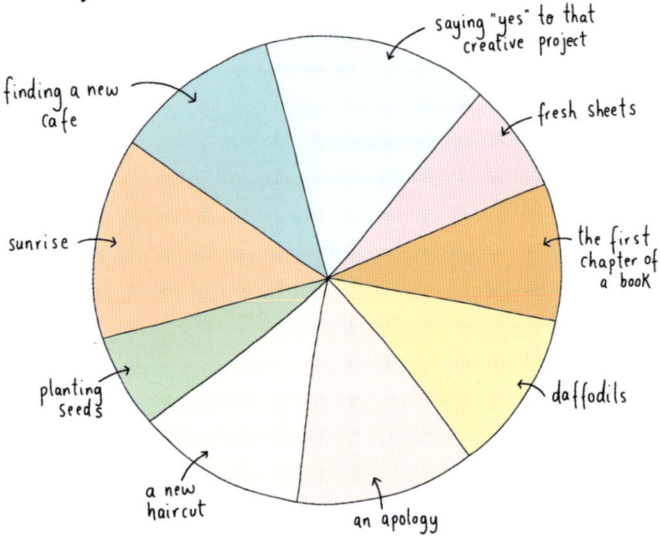

TODAY IS A NEW DAY.

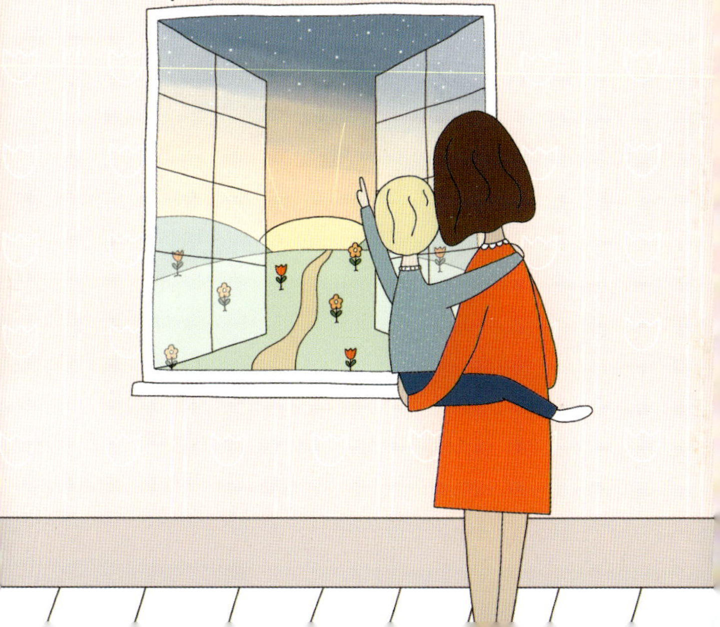

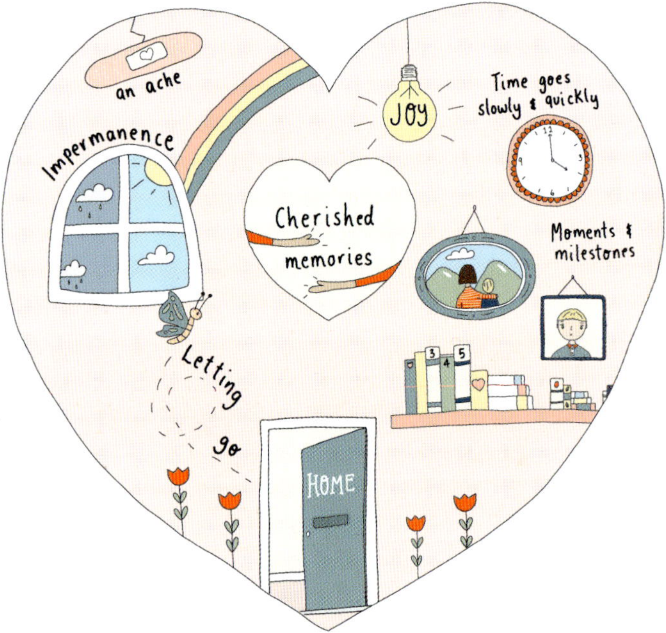
an ache
Impermanence
JOY
Time goes slowly & quickly
Cherished memories
Moments & milestones
Letting go
HOME

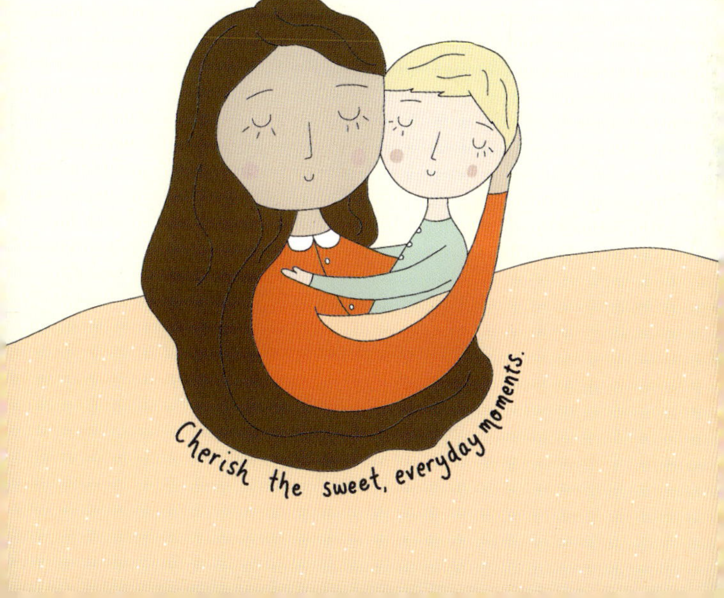
Cherish the sweet, everyday moments.

JOURNAL PROMPTS

Write your thoughts to the prompts below.

What is it that I need today?...

In this moment, I'm looking forward to...

I find comfort in...

Three ways I am growing are...

I feel most myself when...

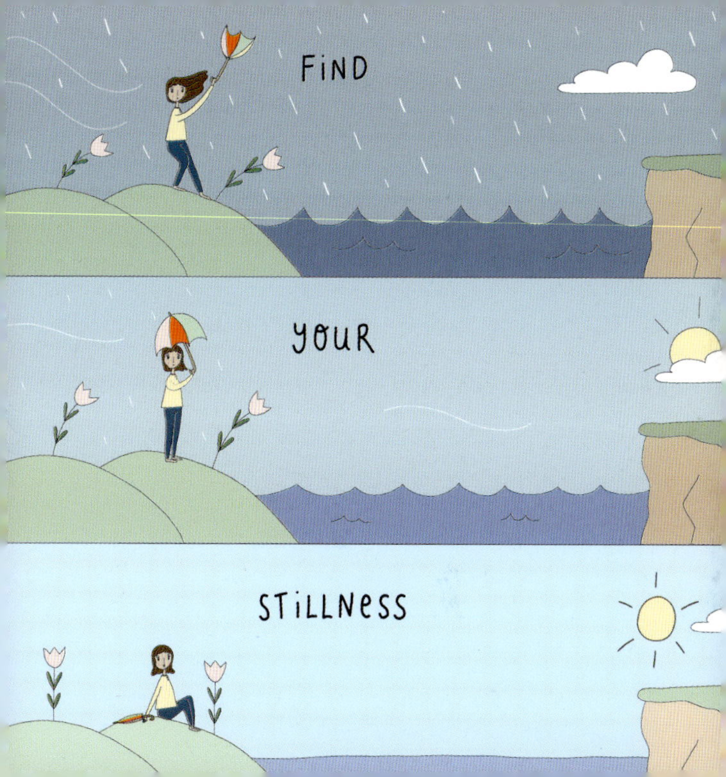
FIND
YOUR
STILLNESS

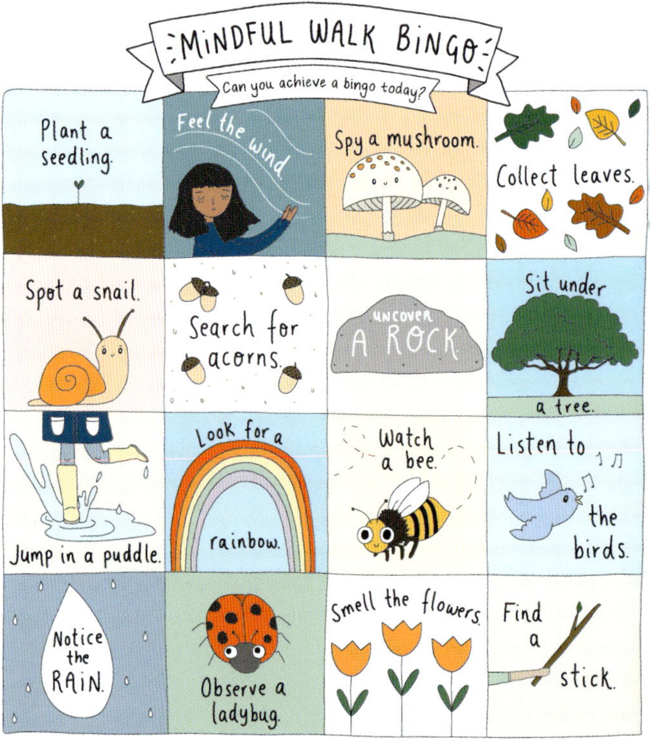
MINDFUL WALK BINGO
Can you achieve a bingo today?
Plant a seedling.
Feel the wind.
Spy a mushroom.
Collect leaves.
Spot a snail.
Search for acorns.
UNCOVER A ROCK.
Sit under a tree.
Jump in a puddle.
Look for a rainbow.
Watch a bee.
Listen to the birds.
Notice the RAIN.
Observe a ladybug.
Smell the flowers.
Find a stick.

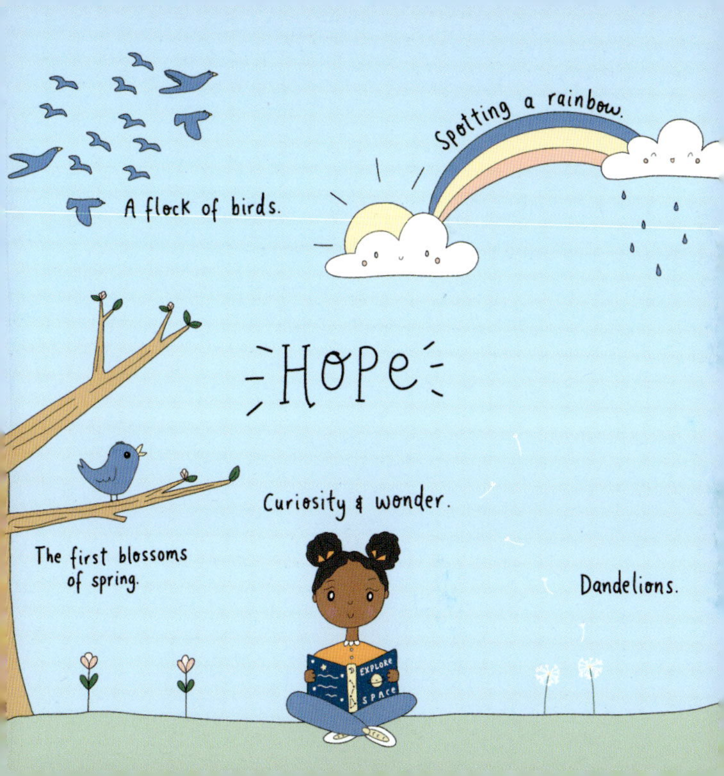
A flock of birds.
Spotting a rainbow.
HOPE
The first blossoms of spring.
Curiosity & wonder.
Dandelions.
EXPLORE SPACE

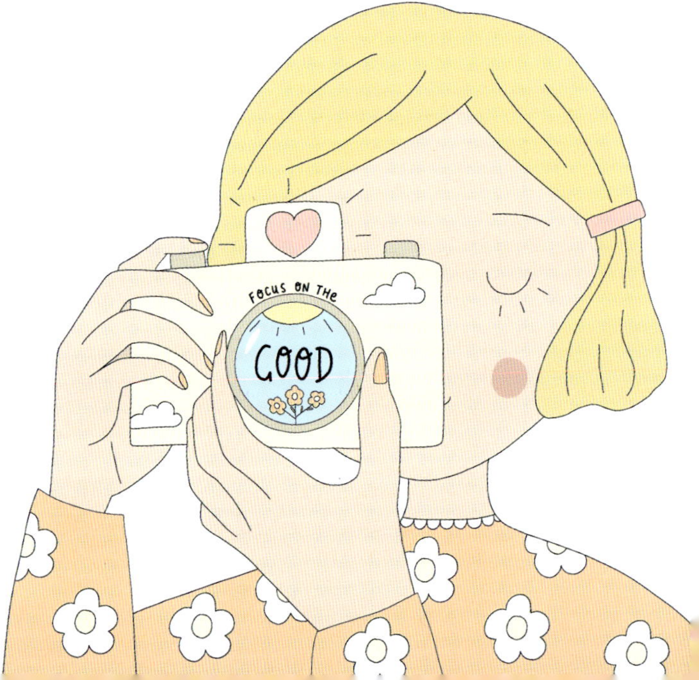
FOCUS ON THE
GOOD

SPREAD HOPE

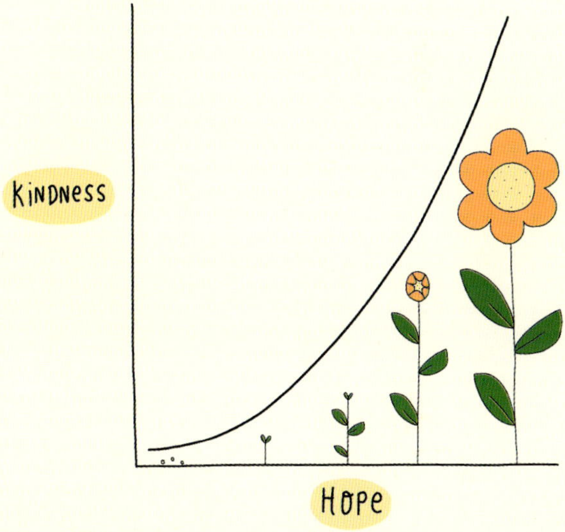

YOU

ARE

NOT

ALONE.

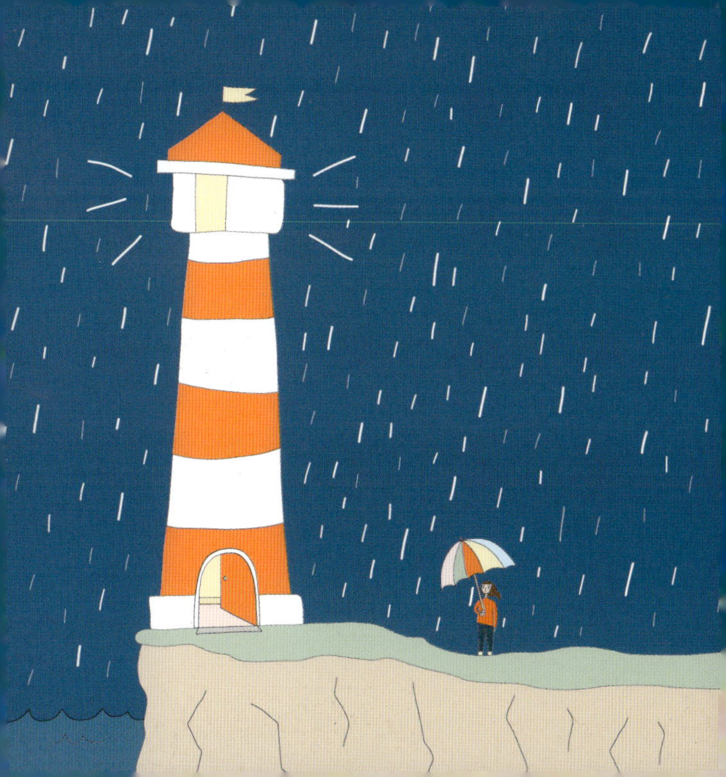

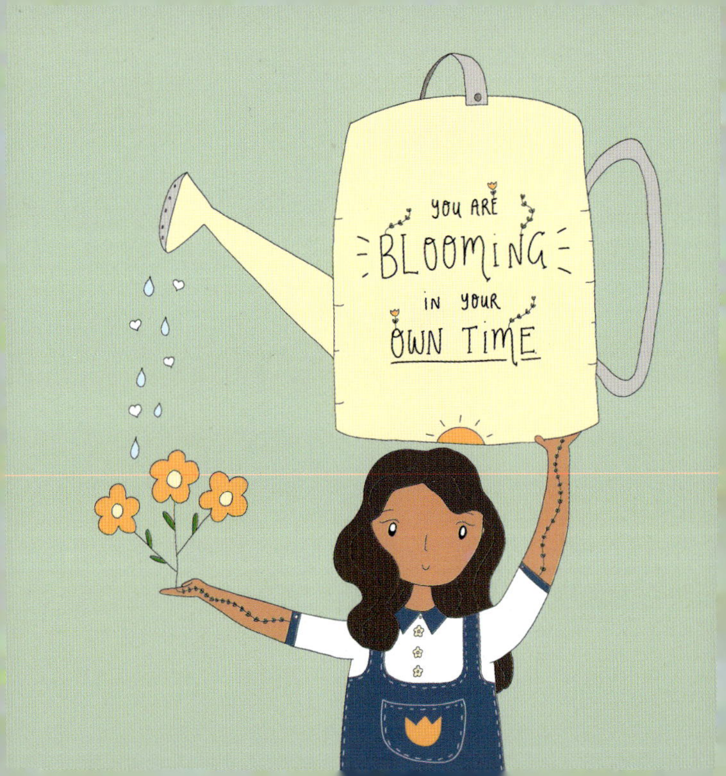

YOU ARE
BLOOMING
IN YOUR
OWN TIME

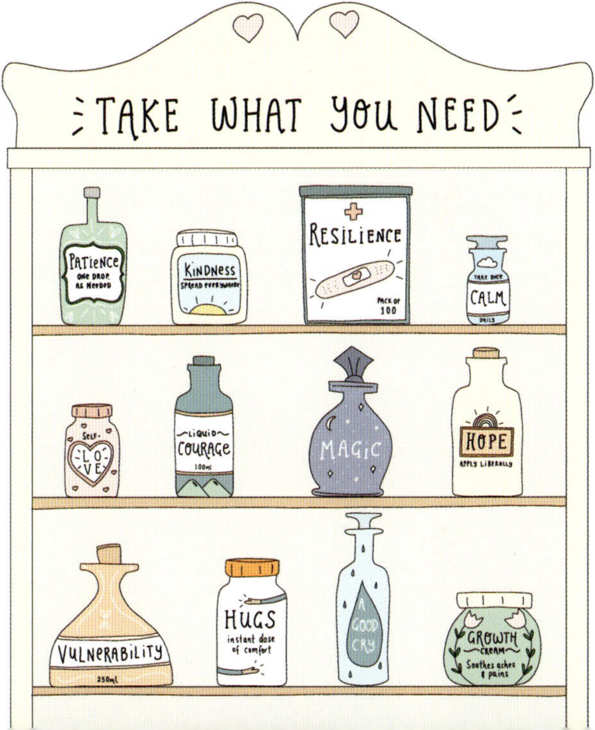
TAKE WHAT YOU NEED
PATIENCE
ONE DROP AS NEEDED
KINDNESS
SPREAD EVERYWHERE
RESILIENCE
PACK OF 100
TAKE ONCE
CALM
DAILY
SELF-LOVE
LIQUID
COURAGE
100ml
MAGIC
HOPE
APPLY LIBERALLY
VULNERABILITY
250ml
HUGS
instant dose of comfort
A GOOD CRY
GROWTH CREAM
Soothes aches & pains

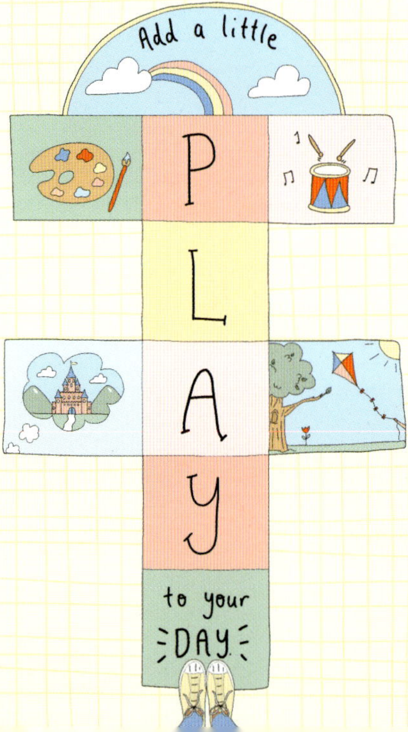
Add a little
PLAY
to your
DAY

Mini Mindfulness

Try a loving kindness exercise! Close your eyes & focus on deep breathing. Say these words to yourself: "May I be happy, may I be healthy, may I be safe, may I be at peace." Then picture someone in your life & say these words to them: "May you be happy, may you be healthy, may you be safe, may you be at peace."

Perspective

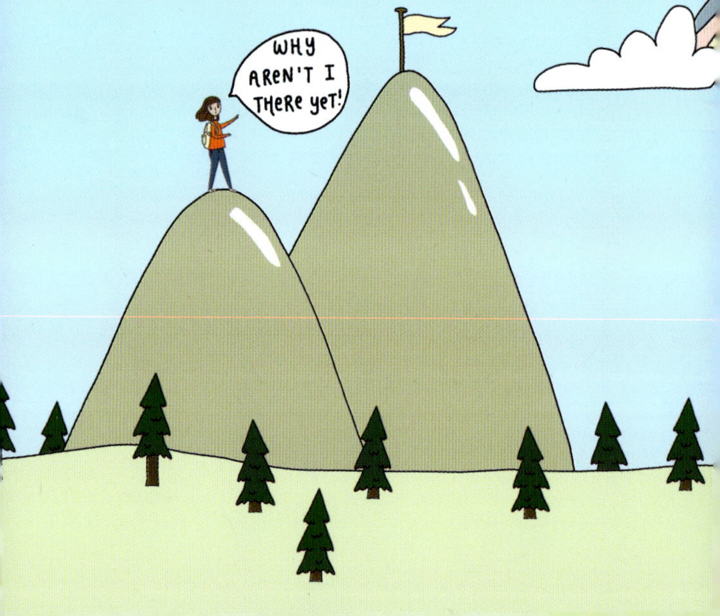

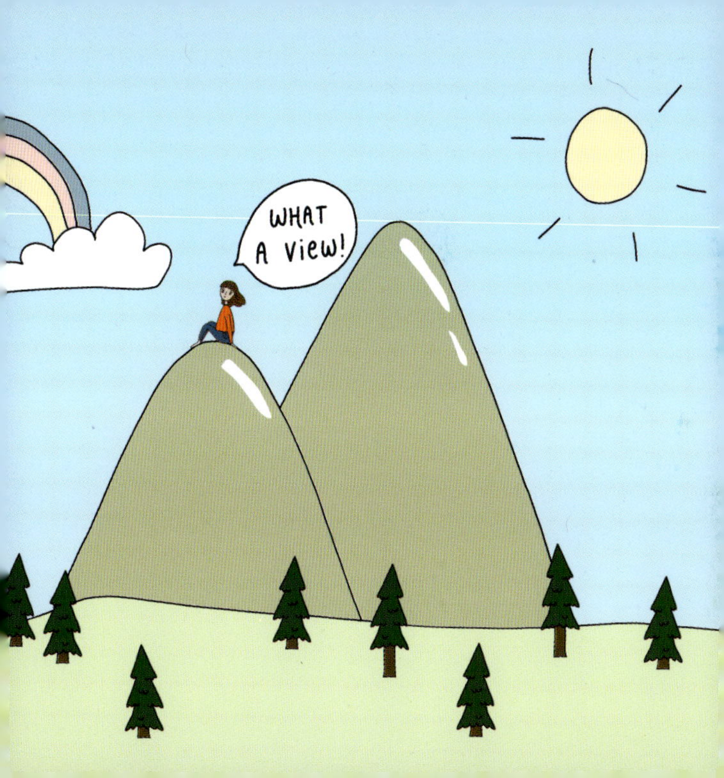
WHAT A VIEW!

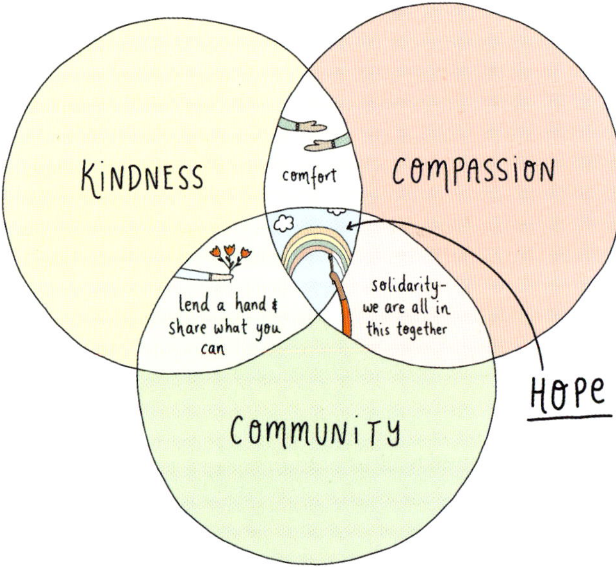
KINDNESS
COMPASSION
COMMUNITY
comfort
lend a hand & share what you can
solidarity-
we are all in this together
HOPE

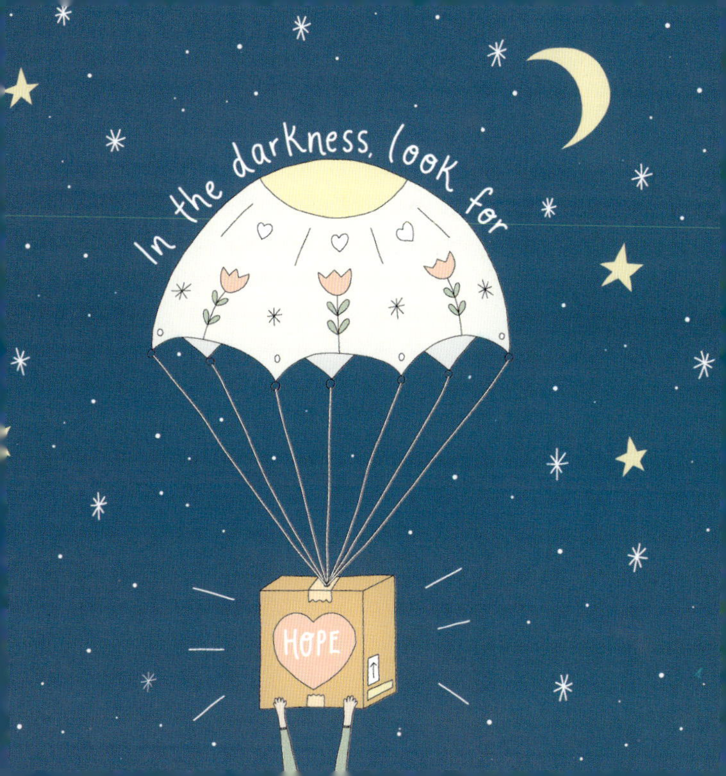
In the darkness, look for
HOPE

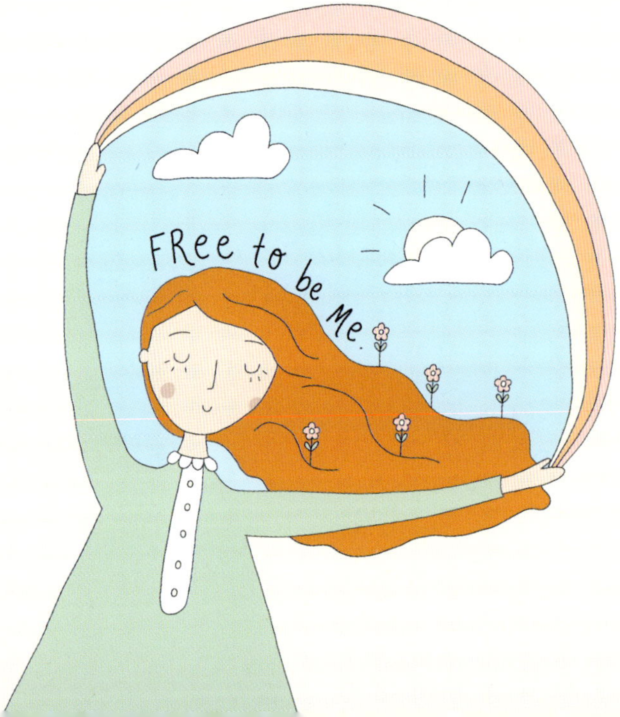
FRee to be Me.

YOU ARE GROWING

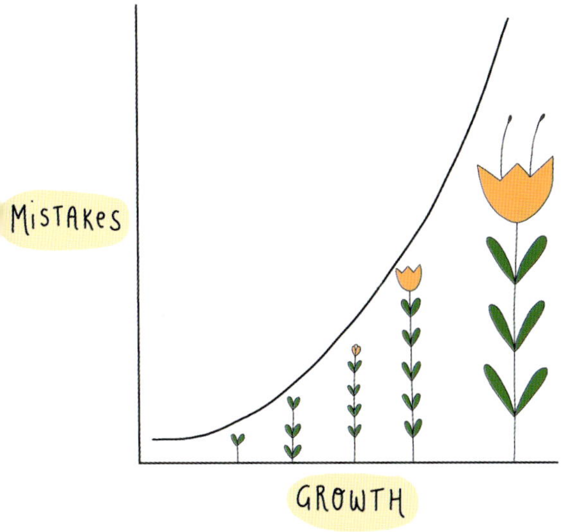

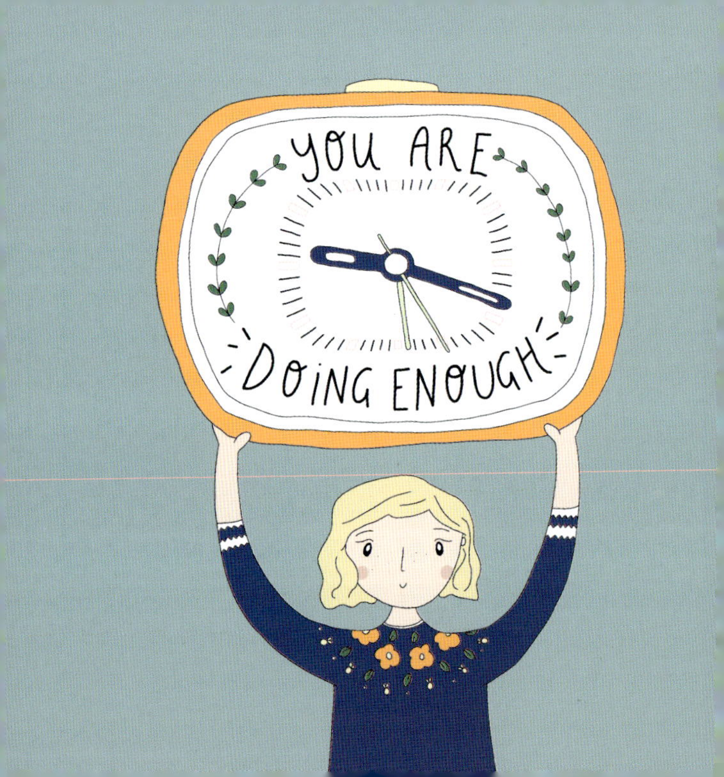
YOU ARE
DOING ENOUGH

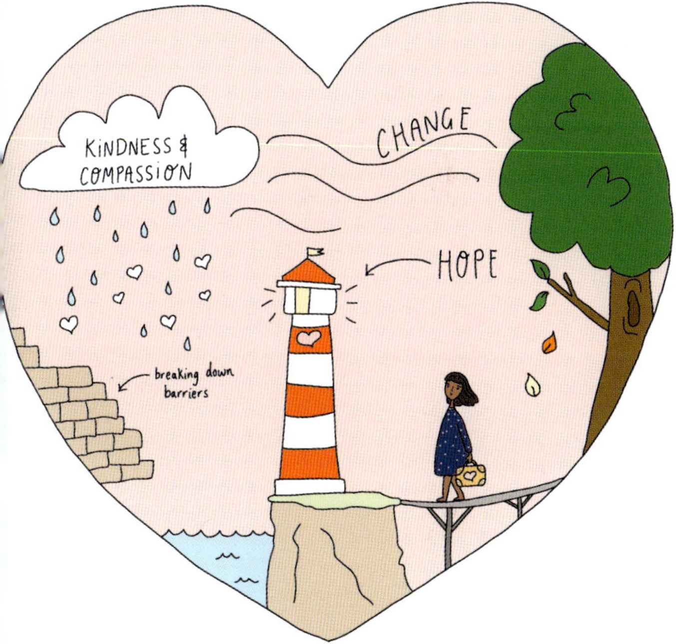
KINDNESS &
COMPASSION
CHANGE
HOPE
breaking down
barriers

REFLECTION

Draw or write about the prompts below.

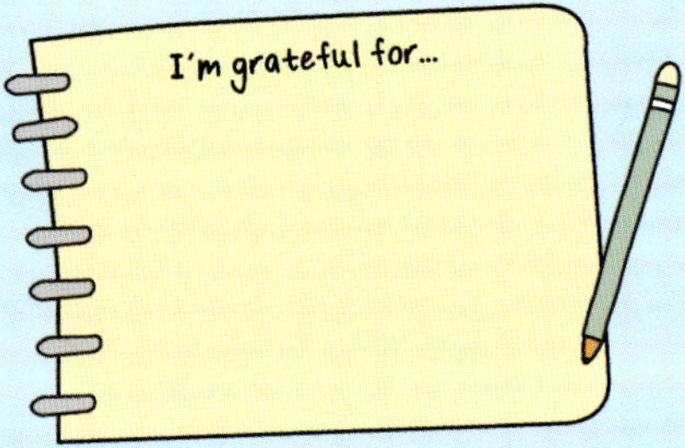

I let go of...

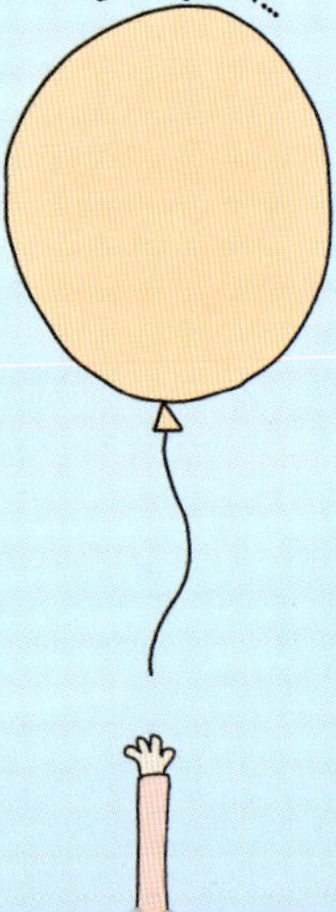

I fill my cup by...

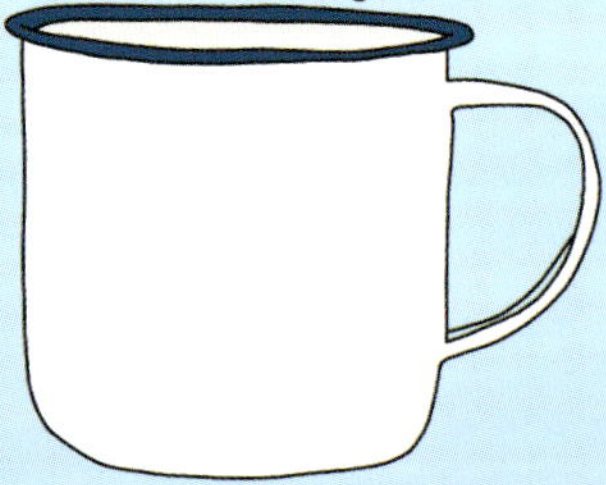

A special memory...

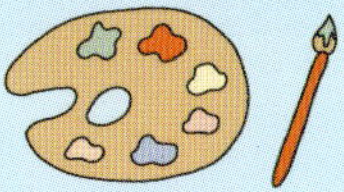

When I was a child, I loved to...

A quote I love...

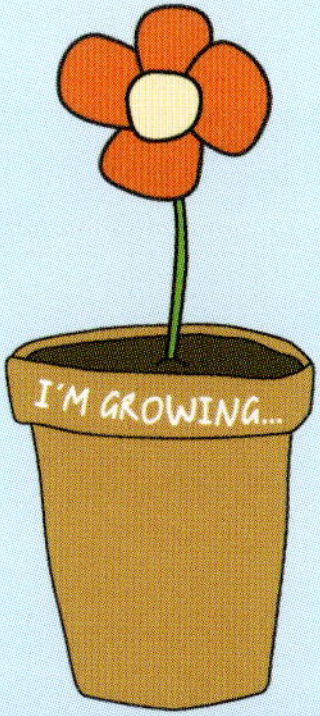

Find what you need:

H	W	O	N	D	E	R	T	F	C	K
J	O	Y	V	T	K	J	R	L	S	I
C	V	P	Q	N	D	T	U	V	Y	N
B	N	V	E	B	H	B	Q	G	B	D
D	Z	J	G	R	O	W	T	H	L	N
H	O	M	E	A	J	H	R	X	O	E
M	V	F	J	V	L	Q	A	K	V	S
X	A	D	V	E	N	T	U	R	E	S
G	Q	P	U	R	P	O	S	E	Z	J

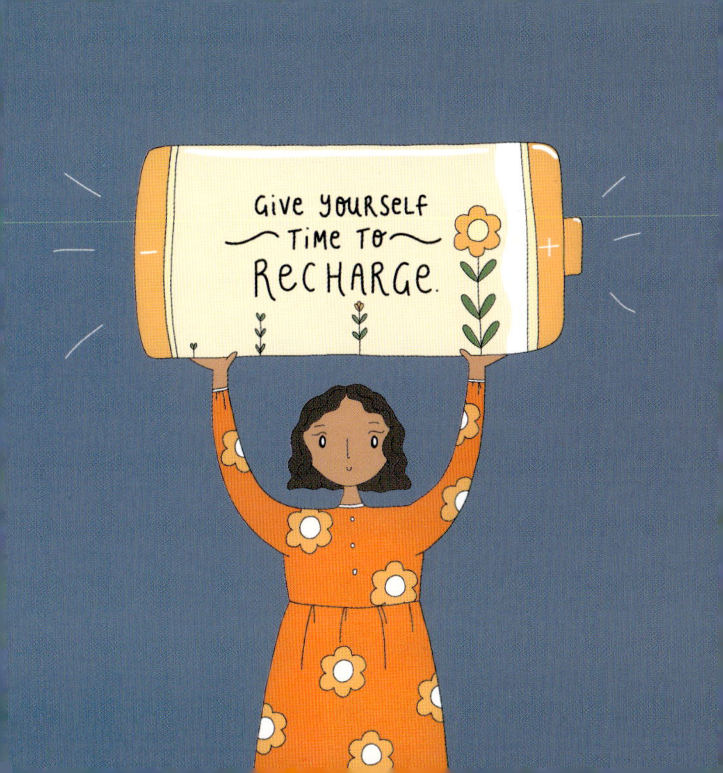
GIVE YOURSELF
TIME TO
RECHARGE.

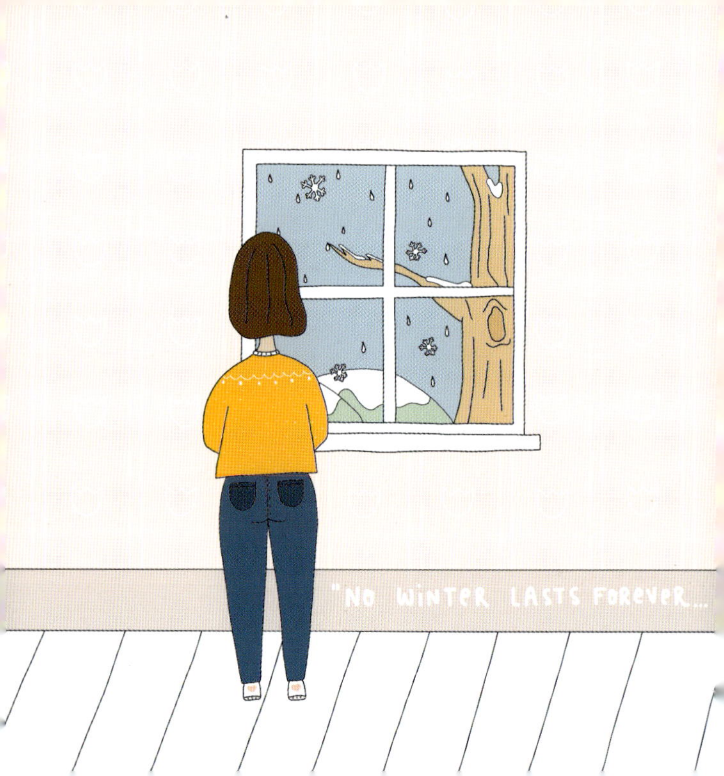
"NO WINTER LASTS FOREVER...

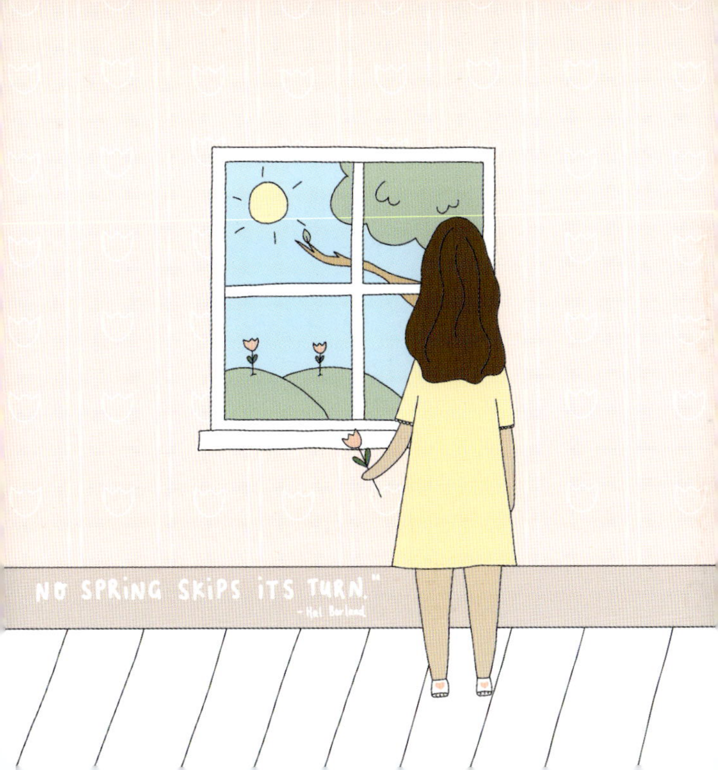
NO SPRING SKIPS ITS TURN."
- Hal Borland

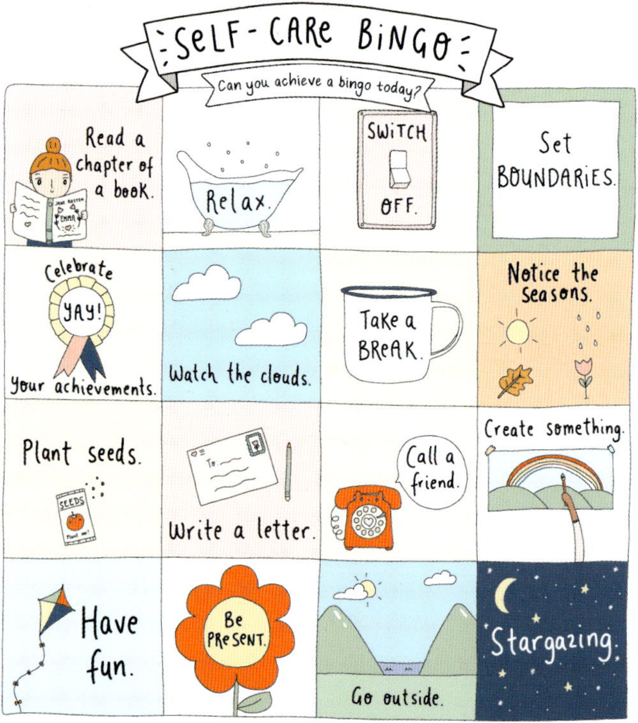
SELF-CARE BINGO
Can you achieve a bingo today?
Read a chapter of a book.
Relax.
SWITCH OFF.
Set BOUNDARIES.
Celebrate your achievements.
YAY!
Watch the clouds.
Take a BREAK.
Notice the seasons.
Plant seeds.
SEEDS
Write a letter.
Call a friend.
Create something.
Have fun.
Be PRESENT.
Go outside.
Stargazing.

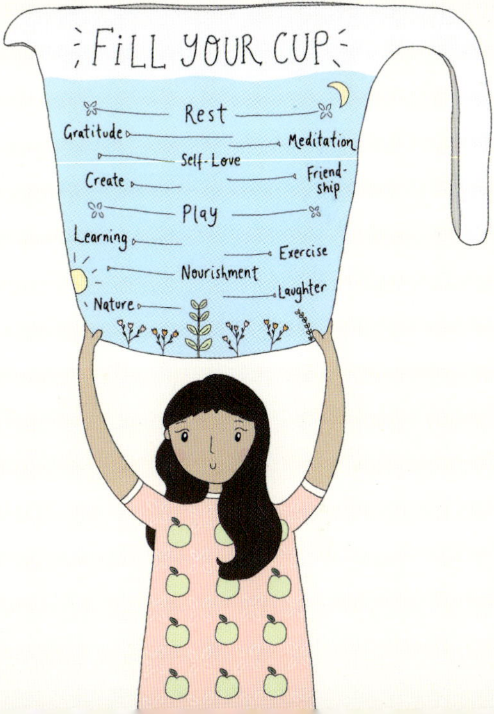
FiLL YOUR CUP
Rest
Gratitude
Meditation
Self-Love
Create
Friendship
Play
Learning
Exercise
Nourishment
Laughter
Nature

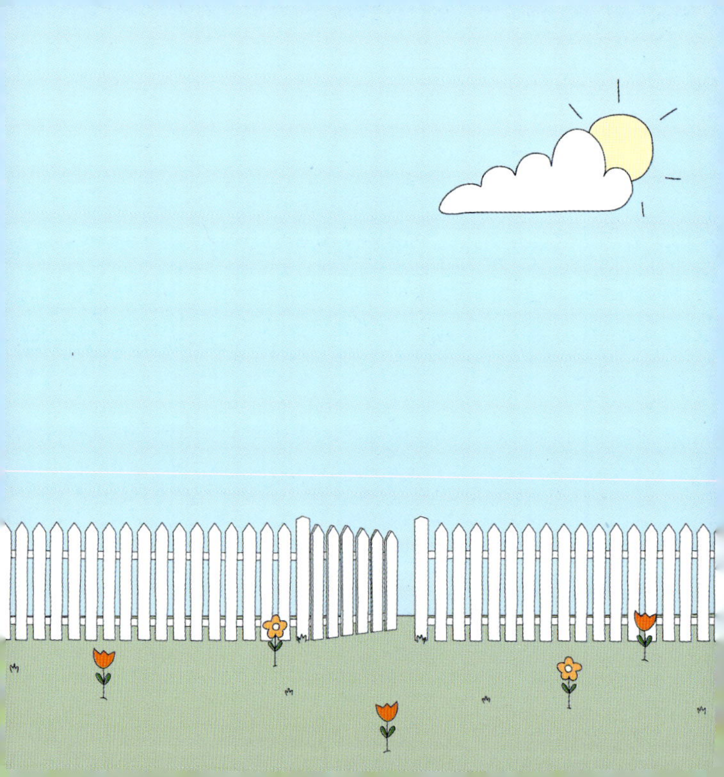

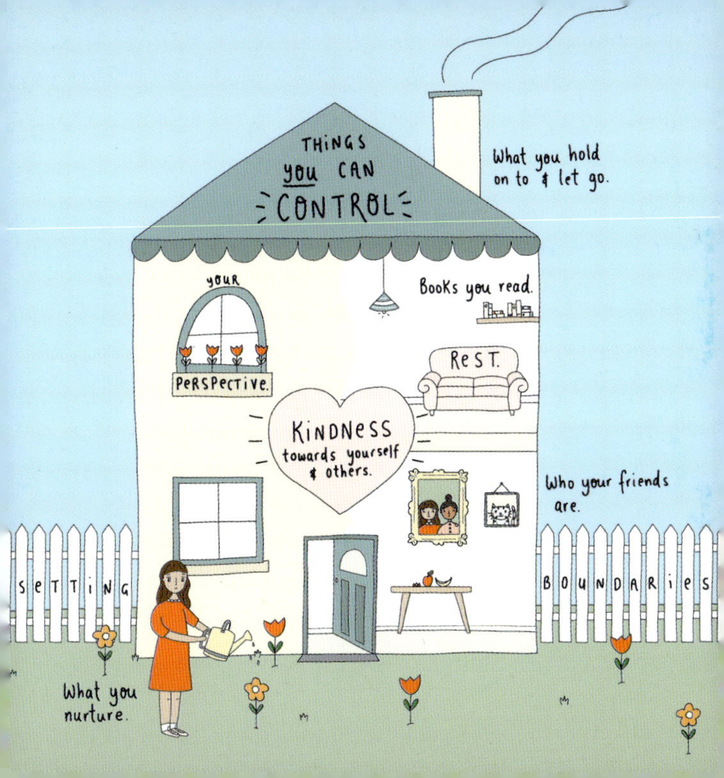
THINGS YOU CAN CONTROL
What you hold on to & let go.
YOUR PERSPECTIVE.
Books you read.
REST.
KINDNESS towards yourself & others.
Who your friends are.
SETTING BOUNDARIES
What you nurture.

OVERTHINKING

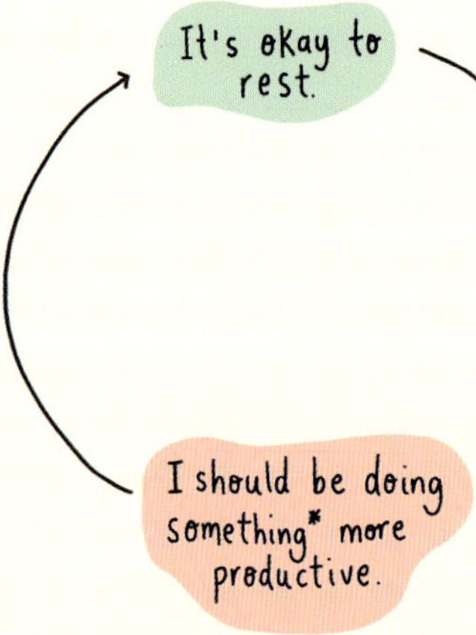

* LIKE UNLOADING THE DISHWASHER, FOLDING THAT PILE OF LAUNDRY, BAKING BREAD, LEARNING HOW TO CROCHET, OR SLOWING DOWN & KNOWING THAT MAKING TIME TO REST IS PRODUCTIVE TOO.

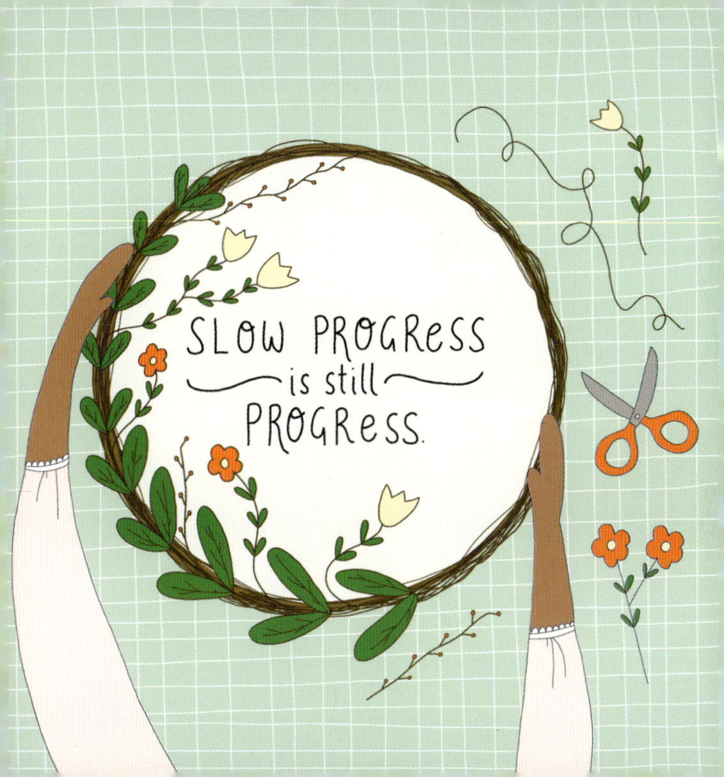
SLOW PROGRESS
is still
PROGRESS.

Mini Mindfulness

It can sometimes feel like our brain is full of thoughts. When you feel like this, try visualizing your thoughts as clouds. Imagine you are sitting on a hill & looking up at your thoughts floating in the sky. Each time you feel a new thought or emotion, create a cloud & push it up out of you & into the sky. Observe your thoughts... & watch them float away.

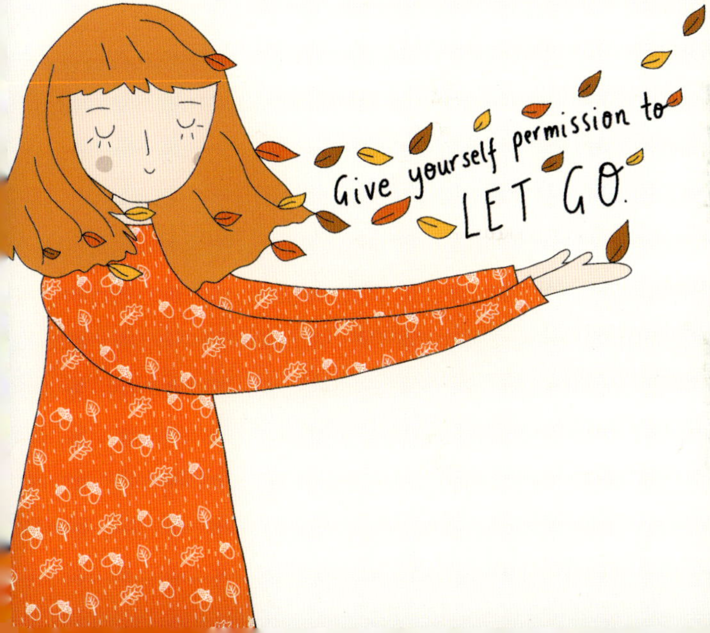
Give yourself permission to
LET GO.

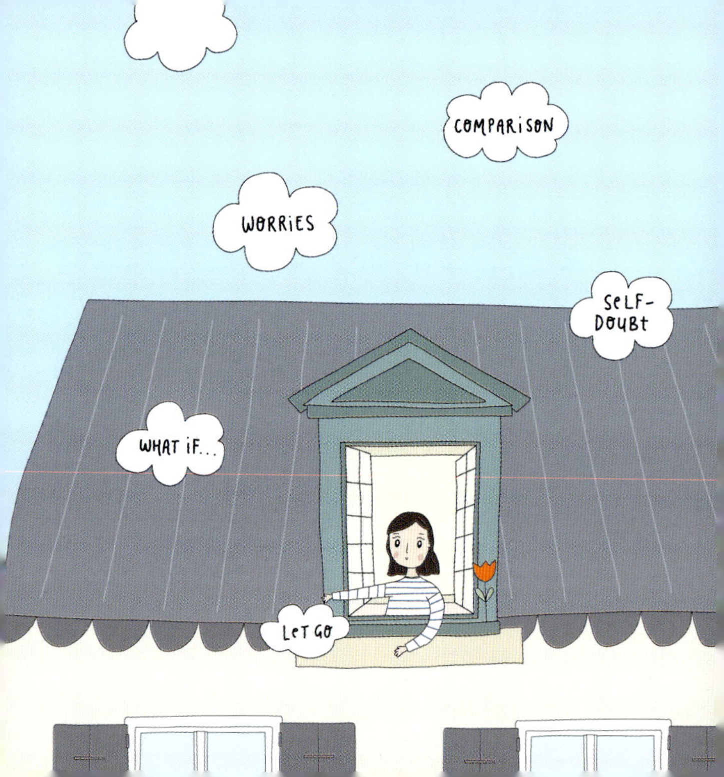
COMPARISON
WORRIES
SELF-DOUBT
WHAT IF...
LET GO

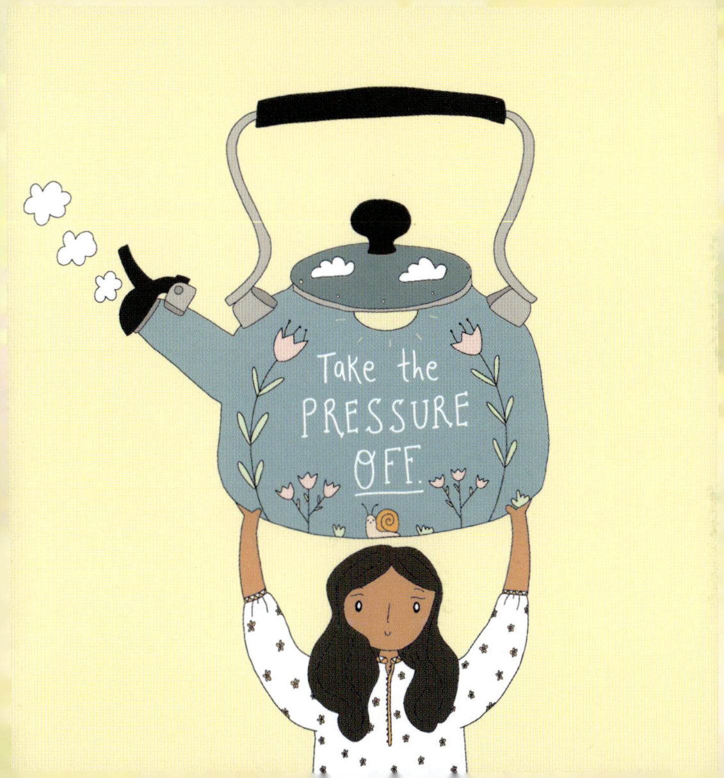
Take the
PRESSURE
OFF.

Resilience

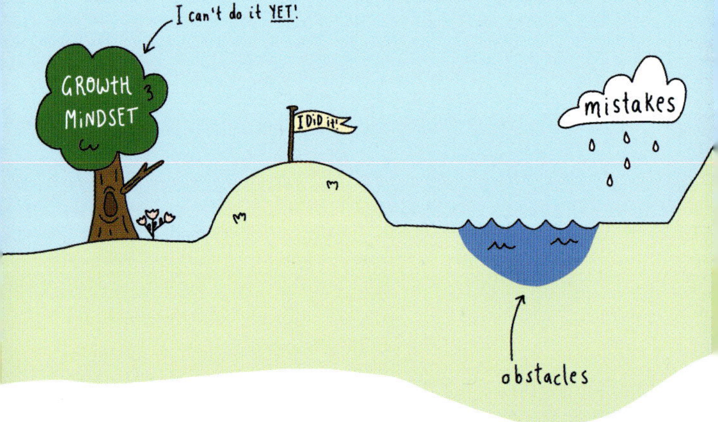

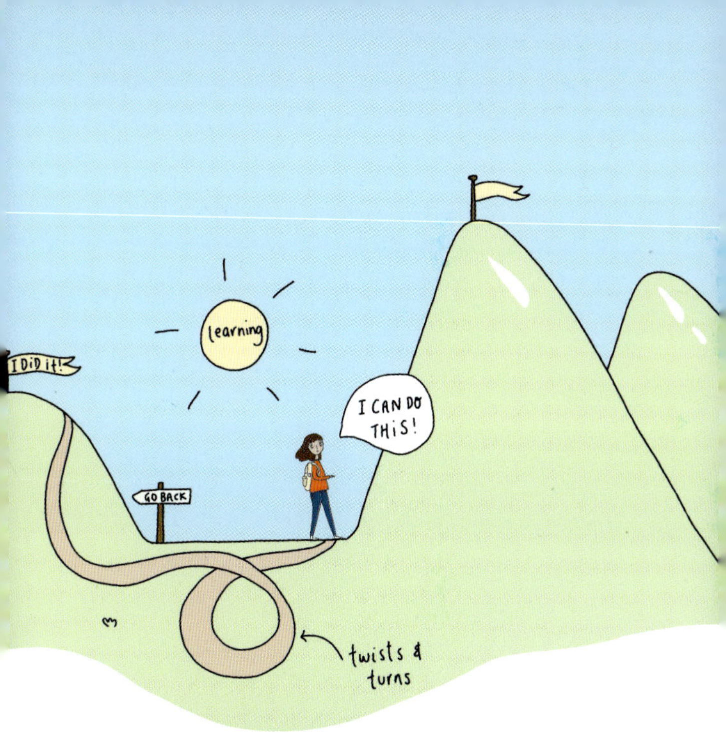
I DID it!
learning
I CAN DO THIS!
GO BACK
twists & turns

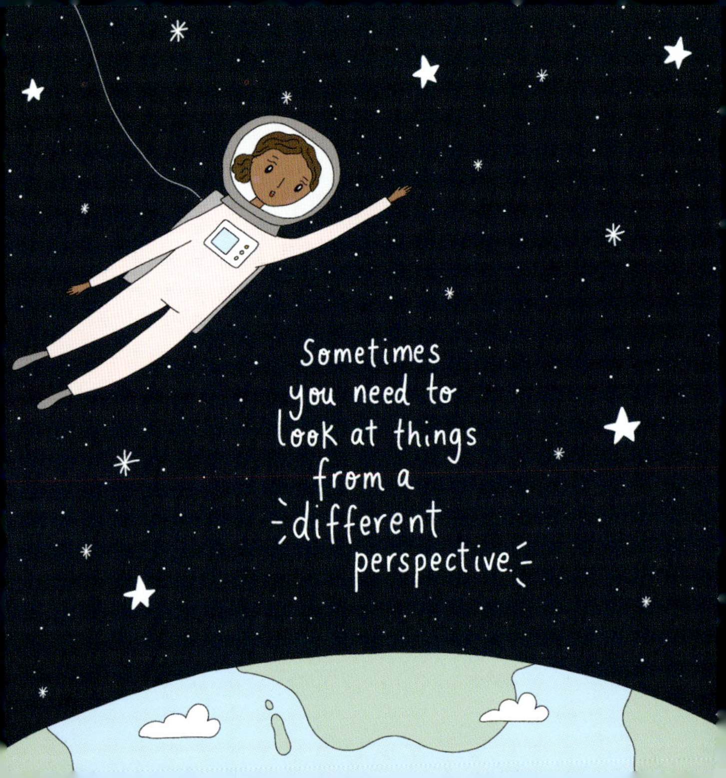
Sometimes you need to look at things from a different perspective.

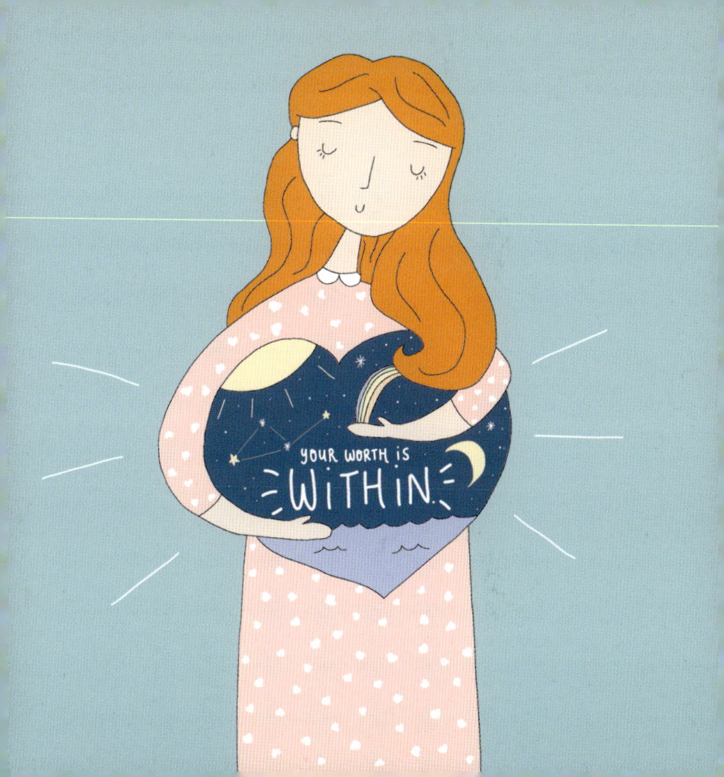
YOUR WORTH IS
WITHIN.

Give Yourself Time

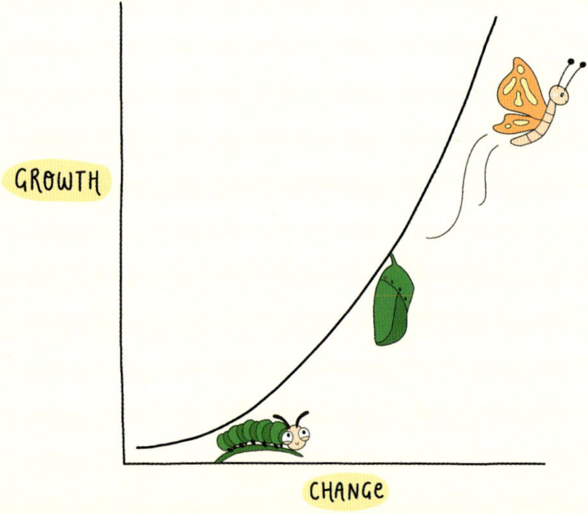

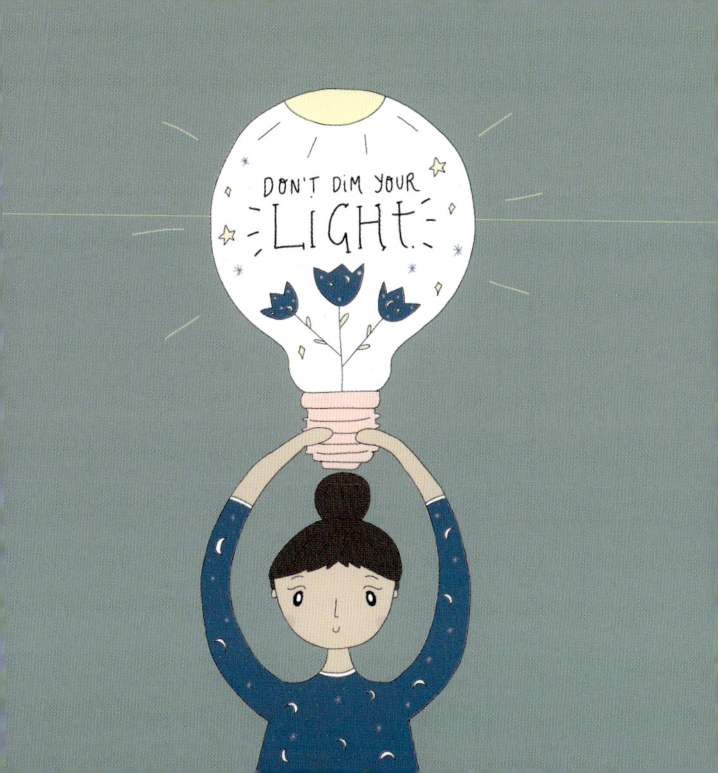
DON'T DIM YOUR
LIGHT.

The greatest painting you can look at is a sky full of stars.

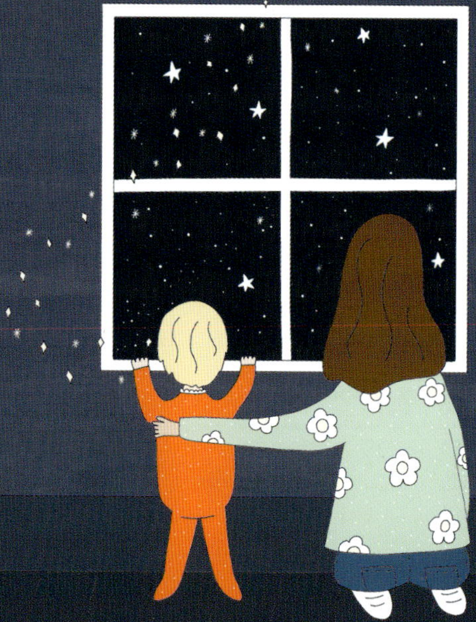

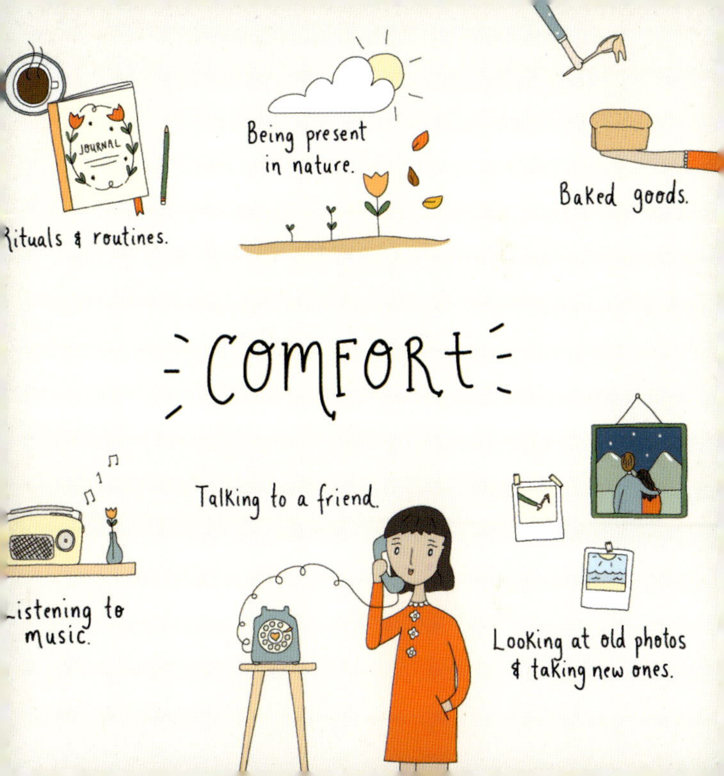
COMFORT
JOURNAL
ituals & routines.
Being present in nature.
Baked goods.
istening to music.
Talking to a friend.
Looking at old photos & taking new ones.

JOURNAL PROMPTS

Write your thoughts to the prompts below.

In these ways, I make time for myself...

To me, new beginnings feel like...

I feel calm when I...

When I reflect on moments of joy, I see...

I celebrate myself by...

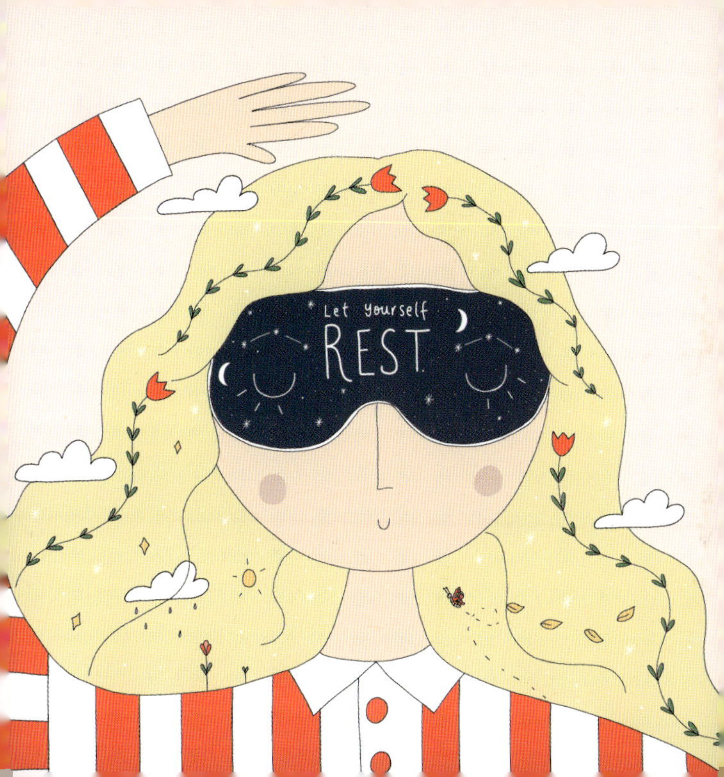
Let yourself
REST

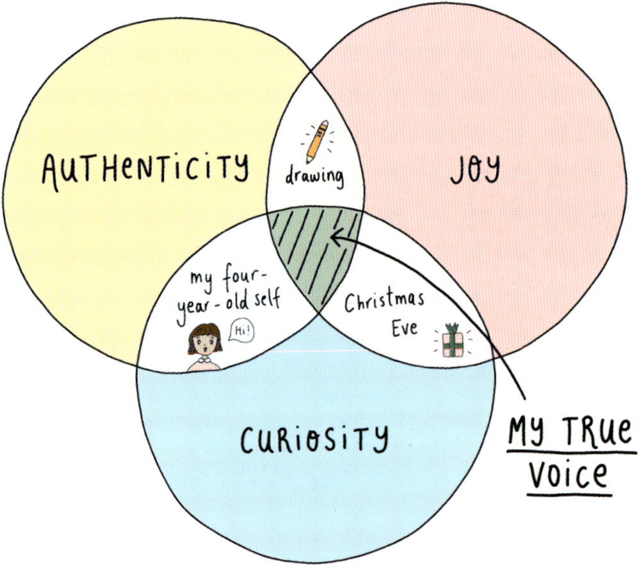
AUTHENTICITY
drawing
JOY
my four-year-old self
Hi!
Christmas Eve
CURIOSITY
MY TRUE VOICE

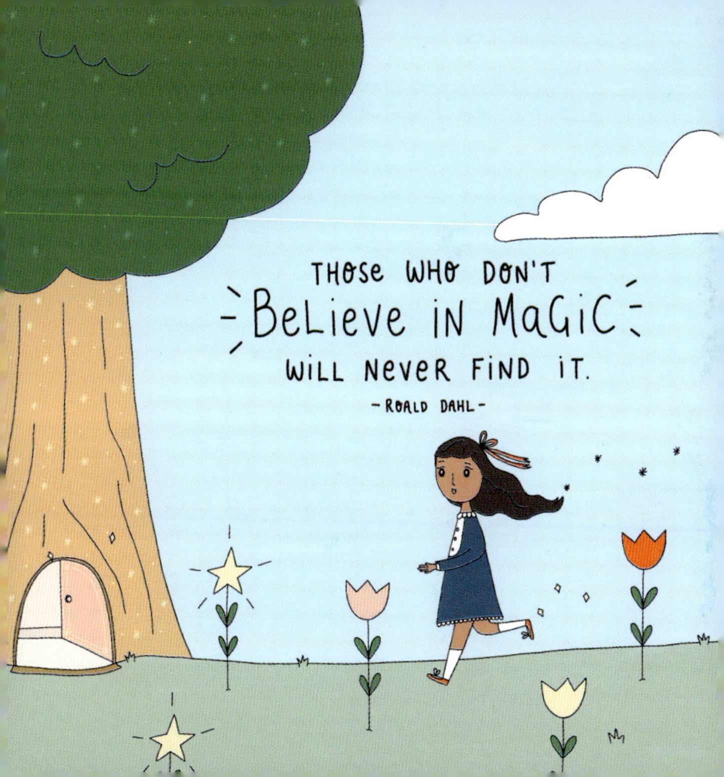
THOSE WHO DON'T
BELIEVE IN MAGIC
WILL NEVER FIND IT.
- ROALD DAHL -

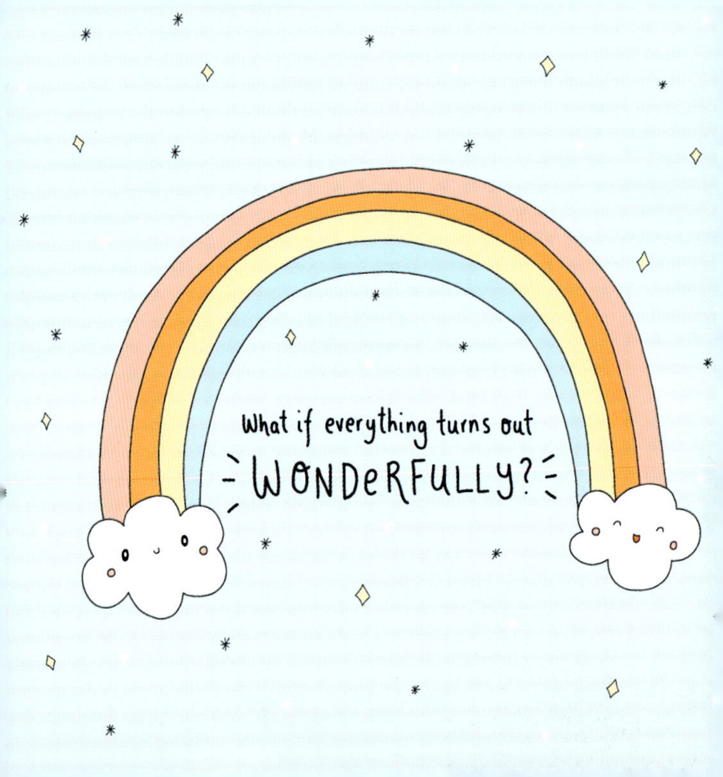
What if everything turns out
WONDERFULLY?

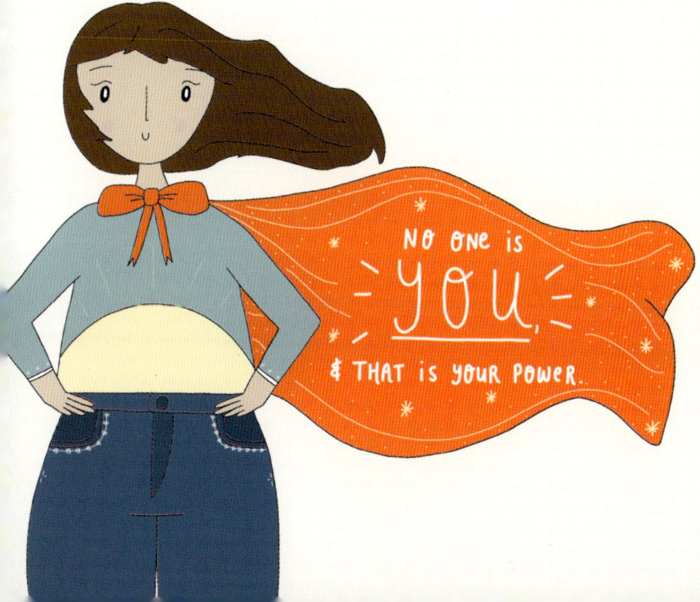
NO ONE IS
YOU,
& THAT IS YOUR POWER.

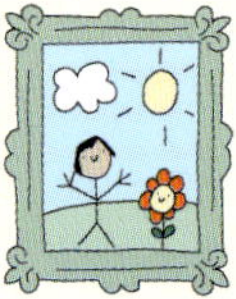

Children's art.

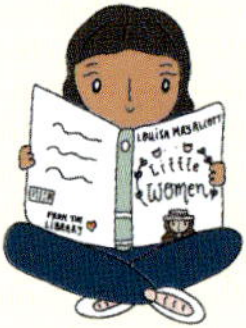

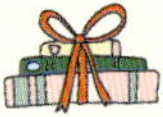

Preloved books.

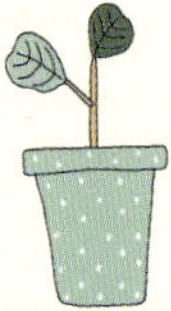

A homegrown plan
or seeds.

SIMPLE GIFTS

Homemade goodies.

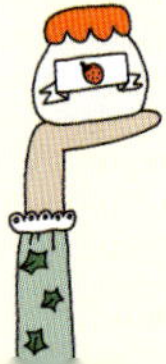

A vintage find.

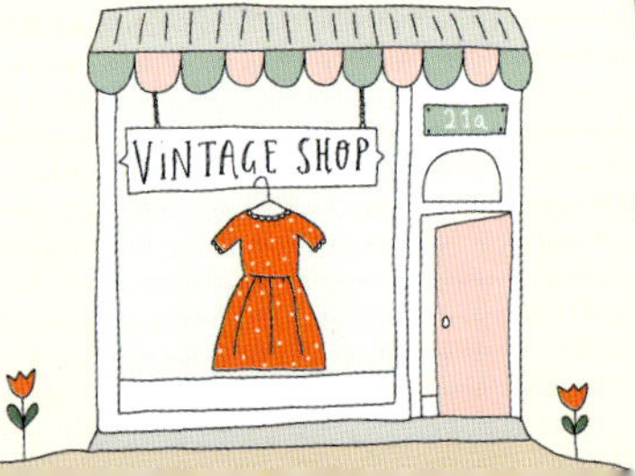

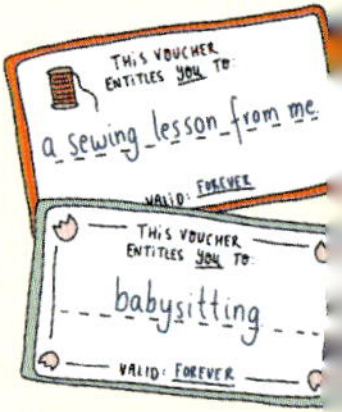

"Vouchers."

Mini Mindfulness

Pick flowers from your garden or while on a walk, then arrange them in a vase or jar. Smell the flowers each morning before you start your day, & spend a moment looking at the intricate petals. You can also do this throughout the day to bring yourself back to the present moment.

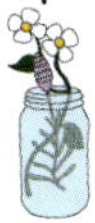

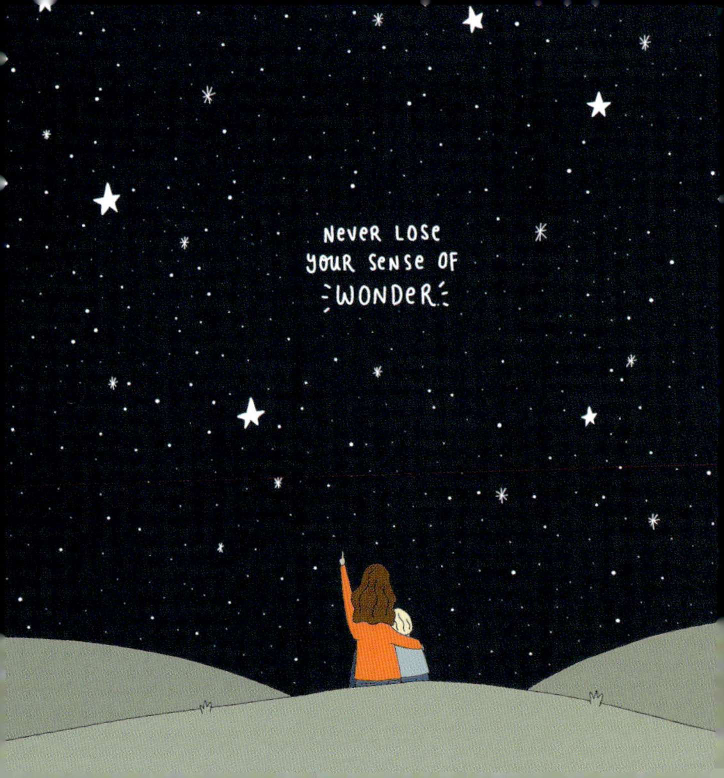
Never lose
your sense of
wonder

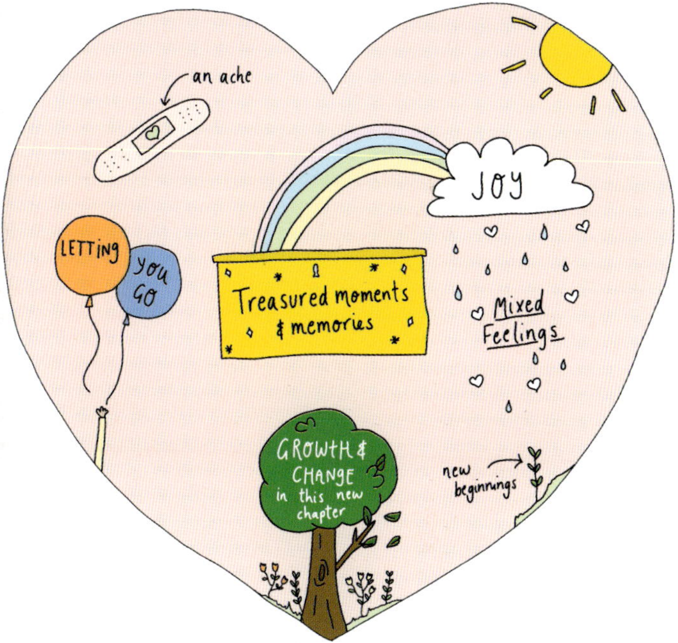
an ache
JOY
LETTING YOU GO
Treasured moments & memories
Mixed Feelings
GROWTH & CHANGE in this new chapter
new beginnings

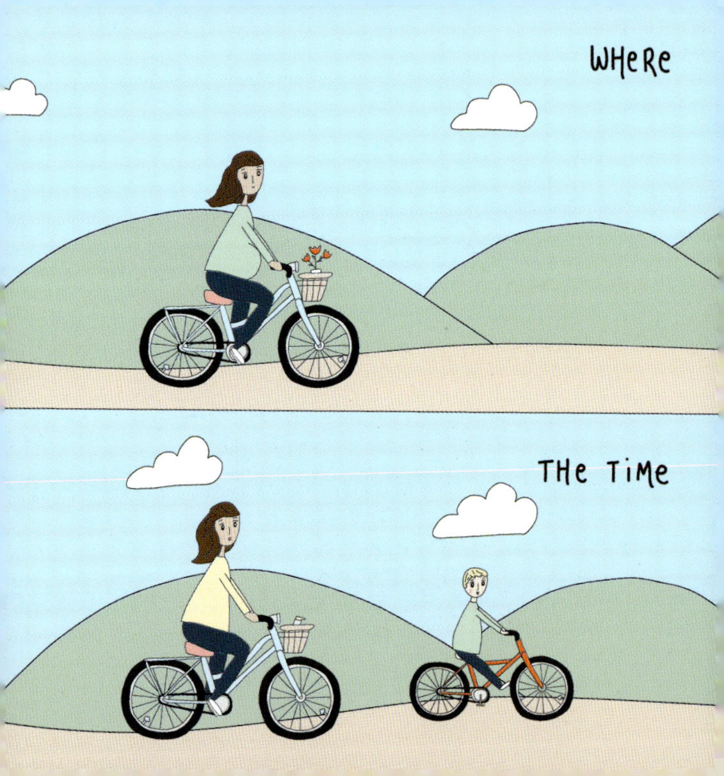
WHeRe
THe Time

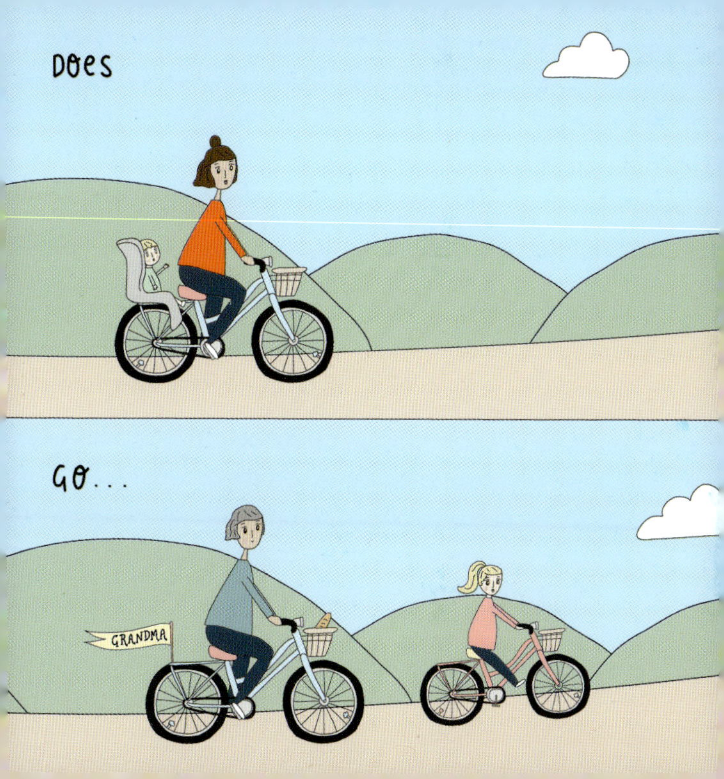
Does
Go...
GRANDMA

SMALL JOYS

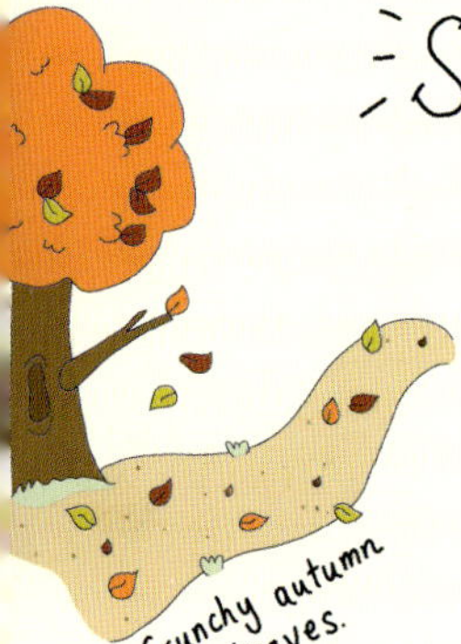

Crunchy autumn leaves.

Reading your favorite childhood book.

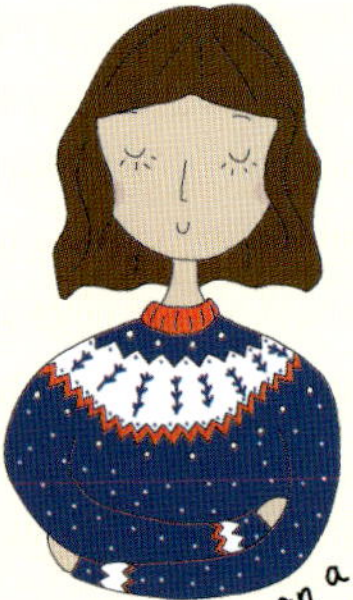

Putting on a cozy sweater.

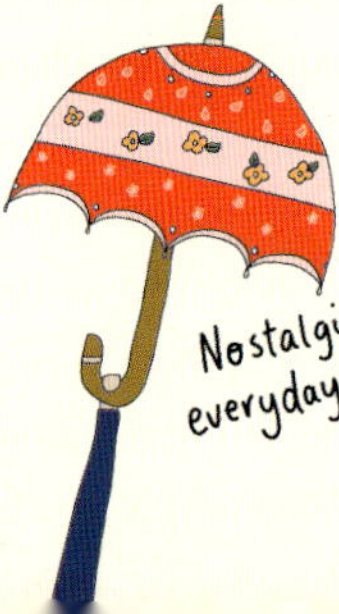

Nostalgic everyday item.

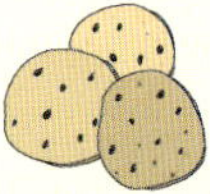

Homemade cookies.

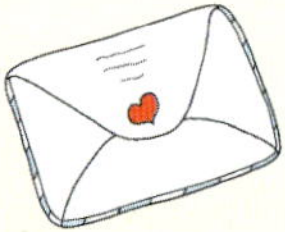

A letter from a friend.

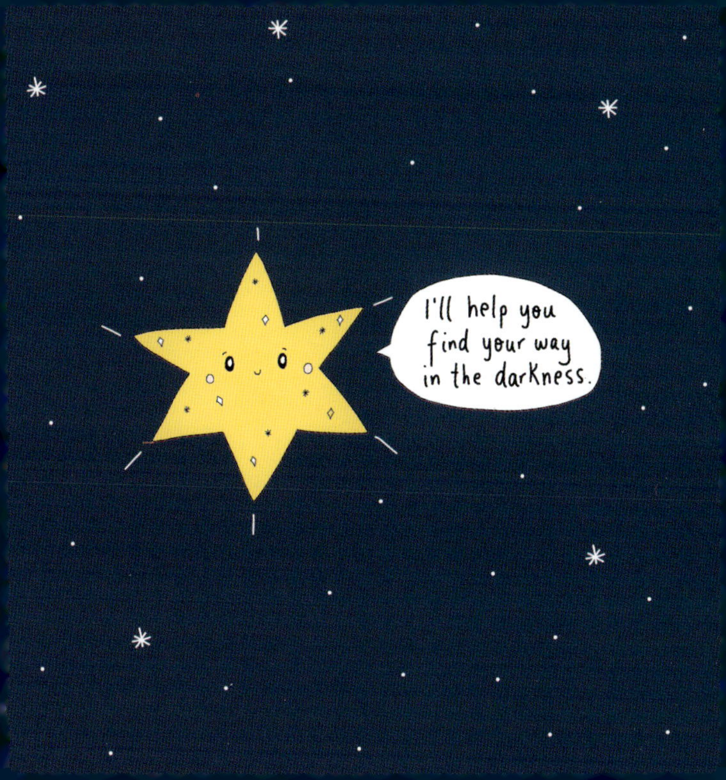
I'll help you find your way in the darkness.

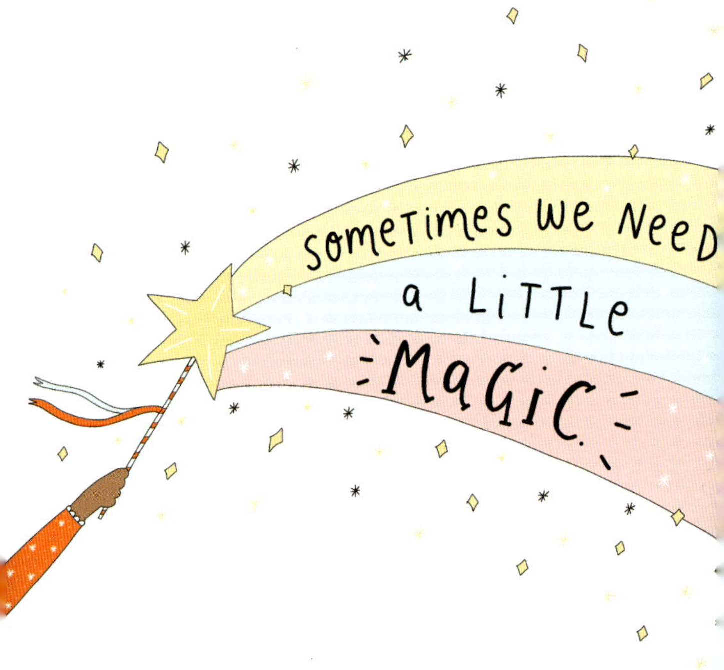
Sometimes we need
a little
Magic

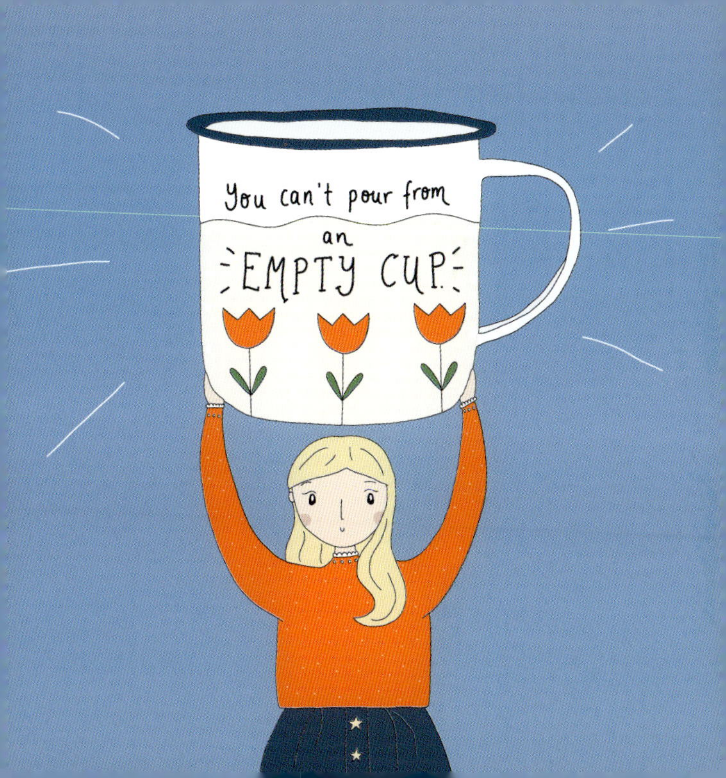
You can't pour from
an
EMPTY CUP.

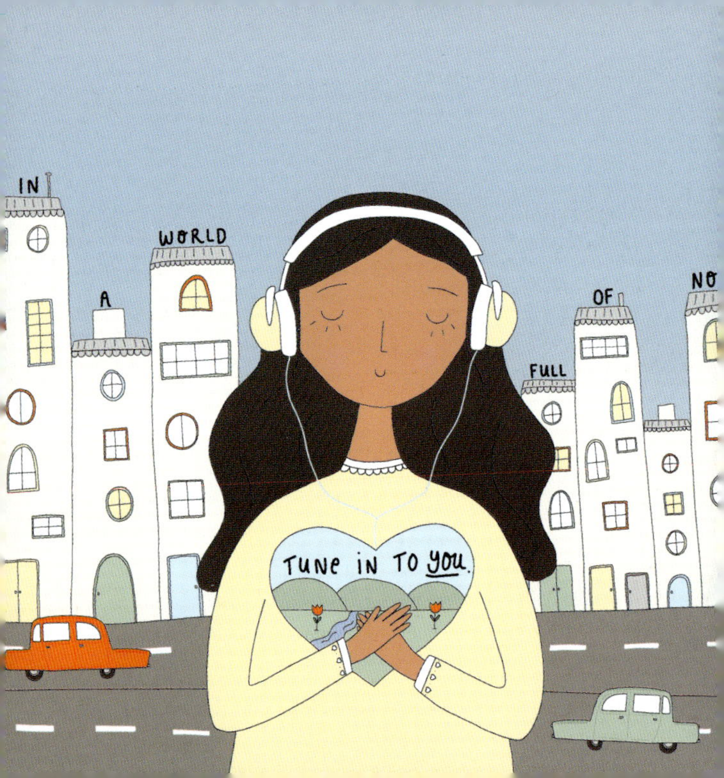
IN
A
WORLD
FULL
OF
NO
TUNE IN TO YOU.

Close your eyes & imagine you are wearing headphones. These headphones tune out the noise & busyness around you. Now, place your hands gently over your heart & slowly breathe in & out, tuning in to you. Take this time to be truly present with yourself.

How do you feel?

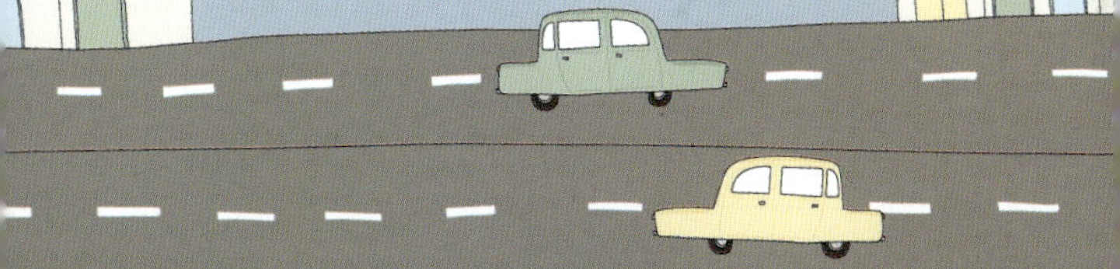

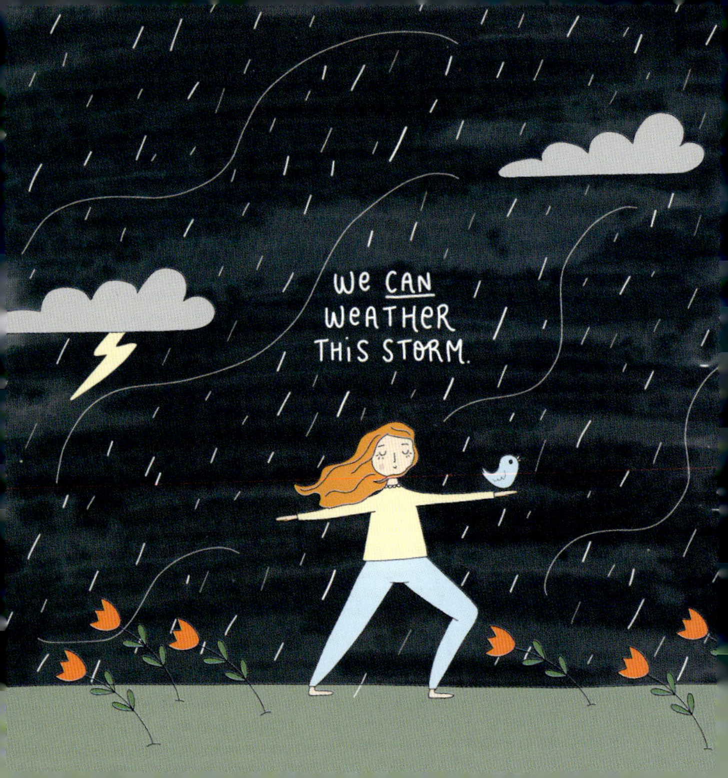
WE CAN
WEATHER
THIS STORM.

TRUST THE PROCESS

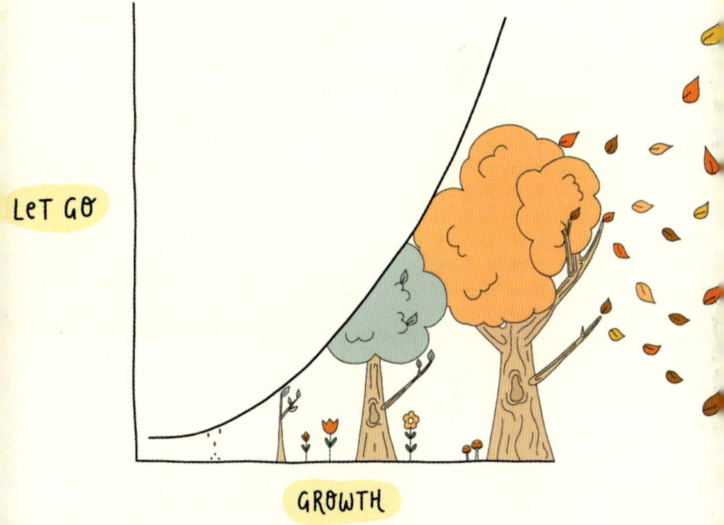

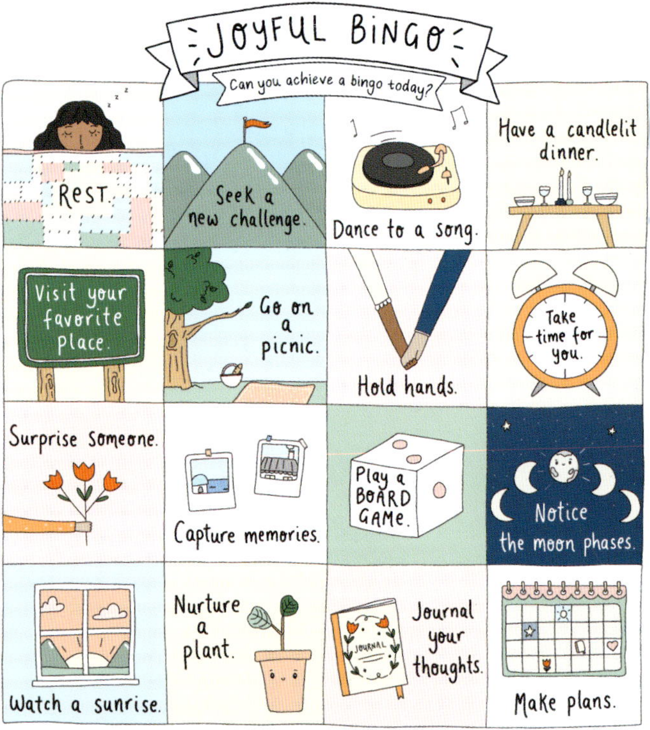
JOYFUL BINGO
Can you achieve a bingo today?
Rest.
Seek a new challenge.
Dance to a song.
Have a candlelit dinner.
Visit your favorite place.
Go on a picnic.
Hold hands.
Take time for you.
Surprise someone.
Capture memories.
Play a BOARD GAME.
Notice the moon phases.
Watch a sunrise.
Nurture a plant.
JOURNAL
Journal your thoughts.
Make plans.

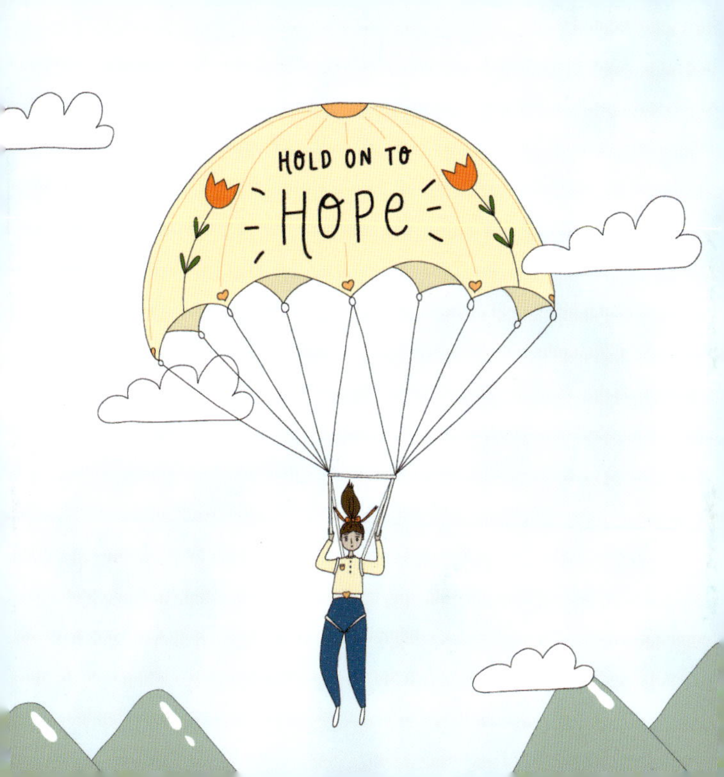
HOLD ON TO
HOPE

Mini Mindfulness

If you are feeling strong emotions, try coming back to your body with deep breathing. Imagine you are holding a flower — now breathe in deeply, like you are smelling it. Then breathe slowly out through your mouth & imagine you are blowing a dandelion, & the seeds are sprinkling through the air.

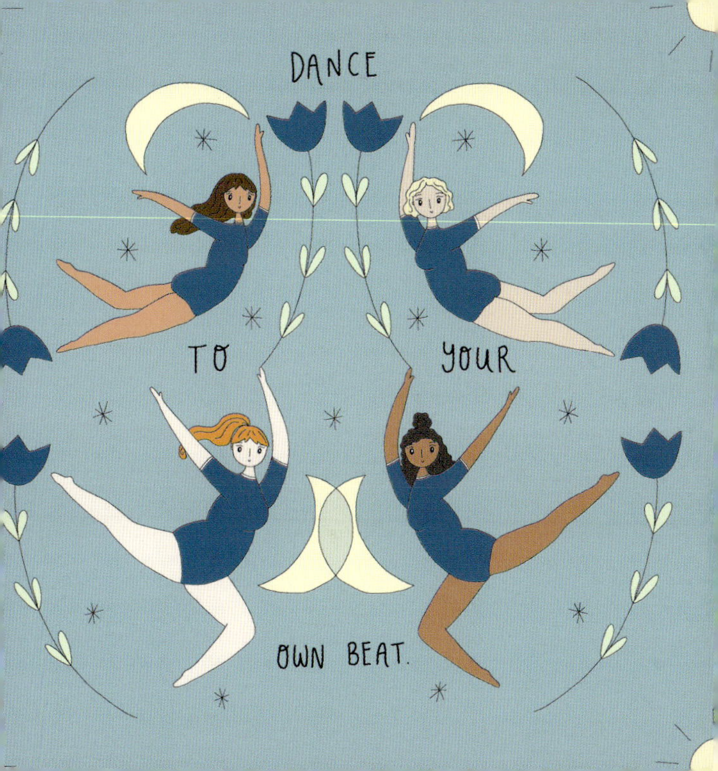
DANCE
TO
YOUR
OWN BEAT.

THE CYCLE

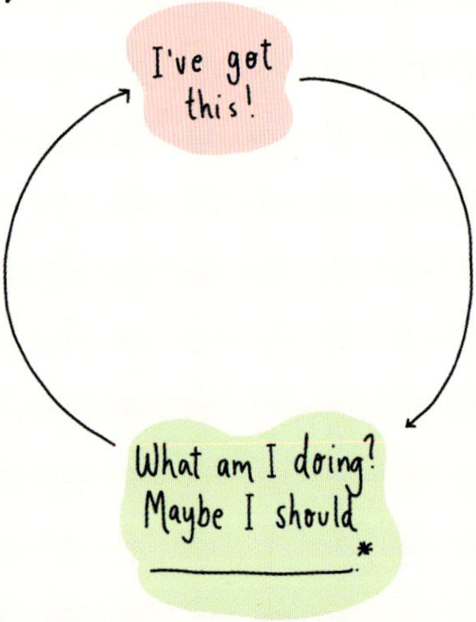

* READ A BLOG POST, SCROLL INSTAGRAM, WATCH NETFLIX, TALK TO A FRIEND, TRY TAROT, JOURNAL, OR JUST QUIET THE NOISE & LISTEN TO MYSELF.

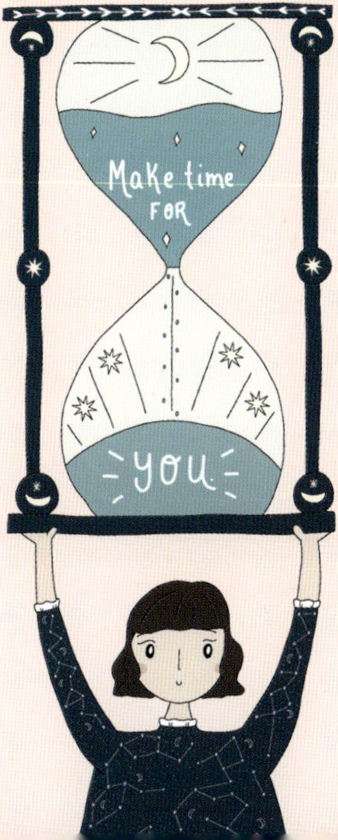
Make time
FOR
YOU

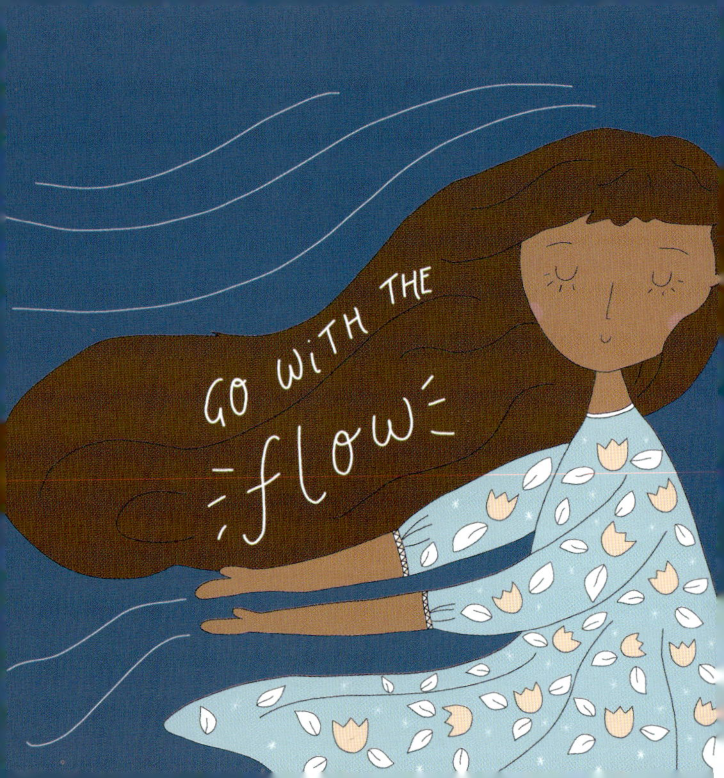
GO WITH THE
flow

You are...

E N O U G H K R J K C
F T Q Y L G V I B P R
S G V L C W N Z V O E
T Q W O R T H Y L W A
R H F V Z M V S Q E T
O Z Q E S A F E V R I
N Y X D J V T Z J F V
G B W C A L M H B U E
D Q A M A Z I N G L F

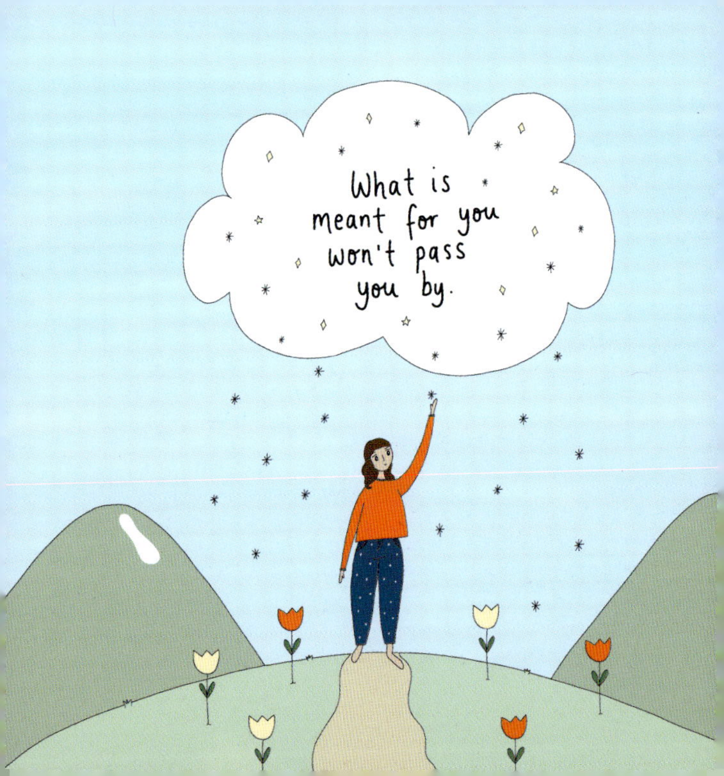
What is meant for you won't pass you by.

ALWAYS BE ON THE LOOKOUT FOR THE PRESENCE OF

WONDER.

-E. B. WHITE-

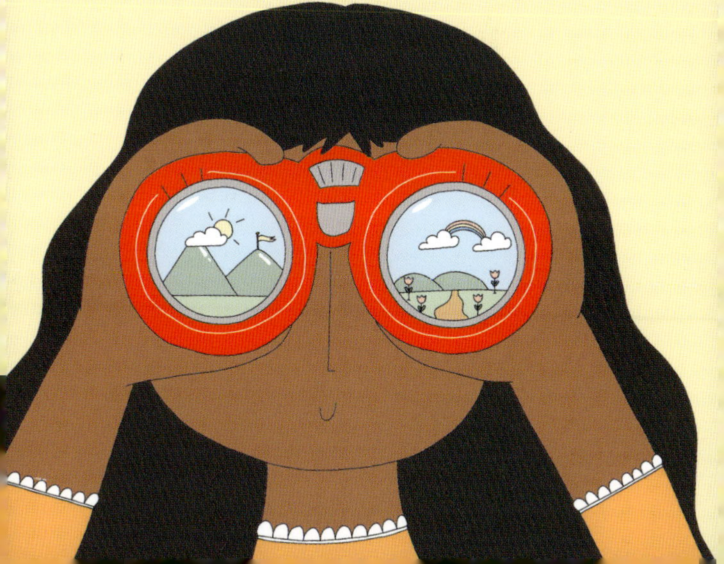

"You are braver than you believe, stronger than you seem, and smarter than you think."

A. A. MILNE

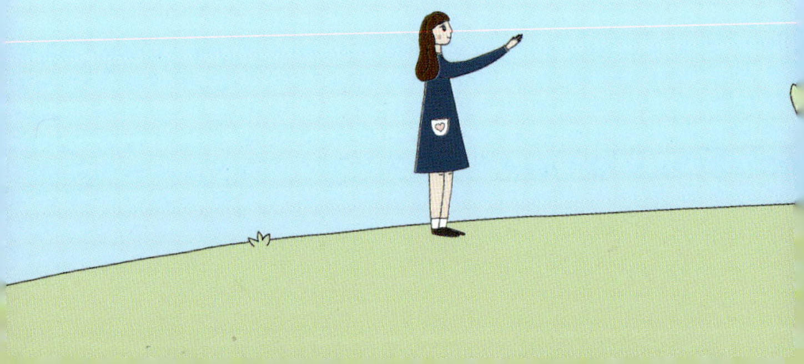

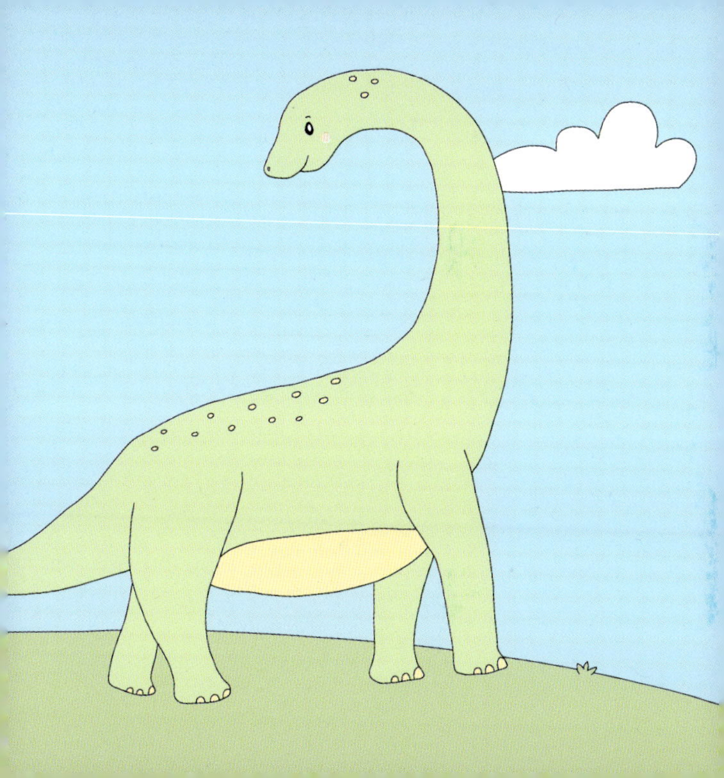

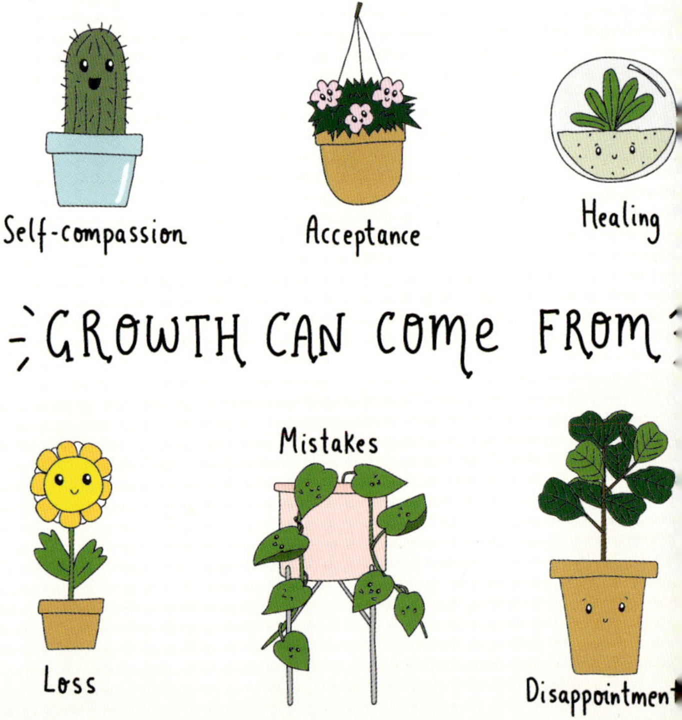
Self-compassion
Acceptance
Healing
GROWTH CAN COME FROM
Mistakes
Loss
Disappointment

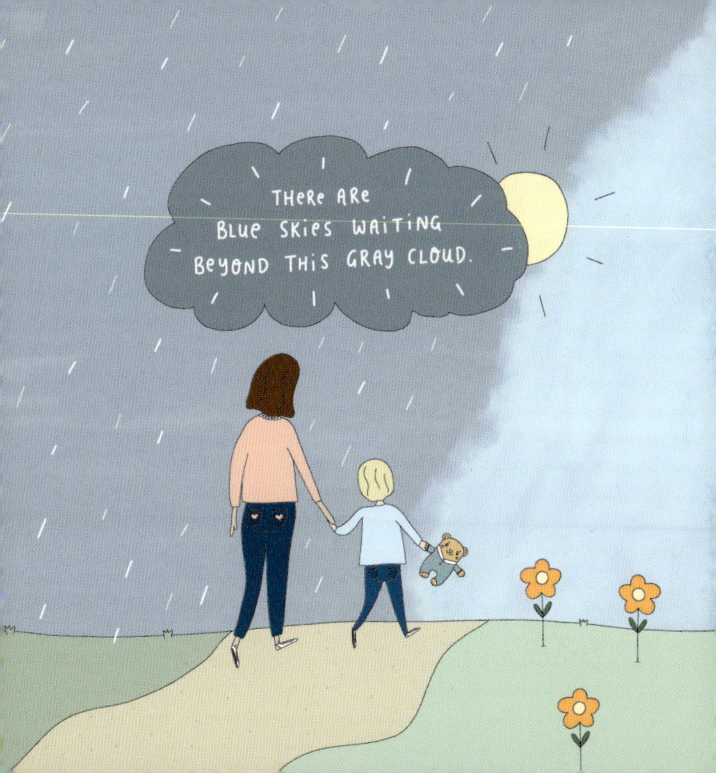
THERE ARE
BLUE SKIES WAITING
BEYOND THIS GRAY CLOUD.

LISTEN TO

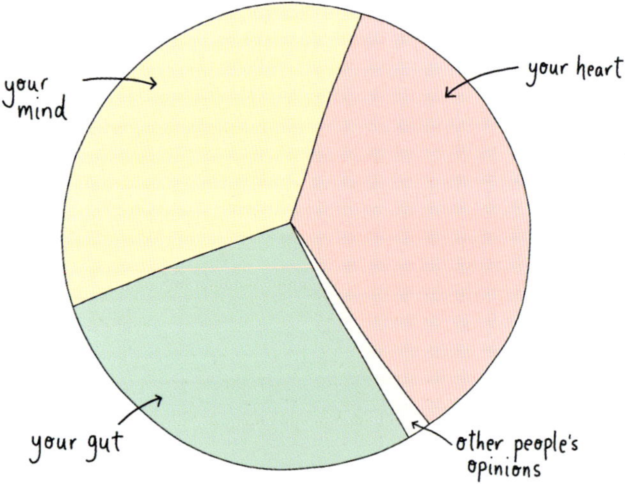

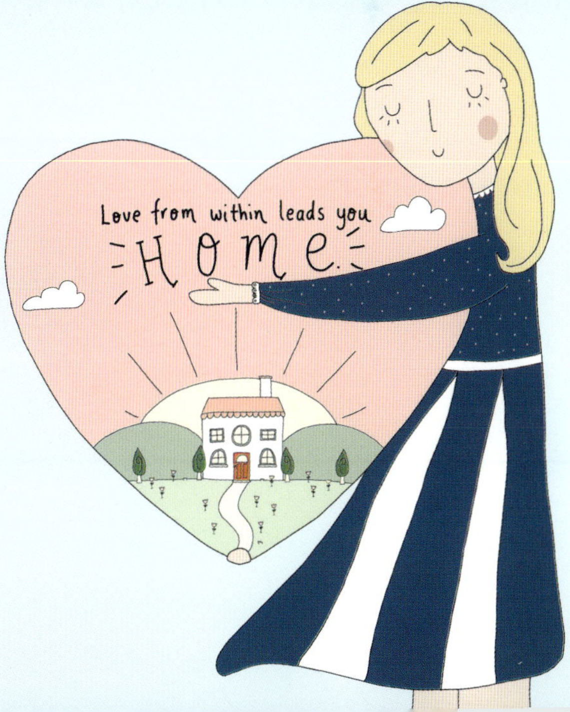
Love from within leads you
HOME.

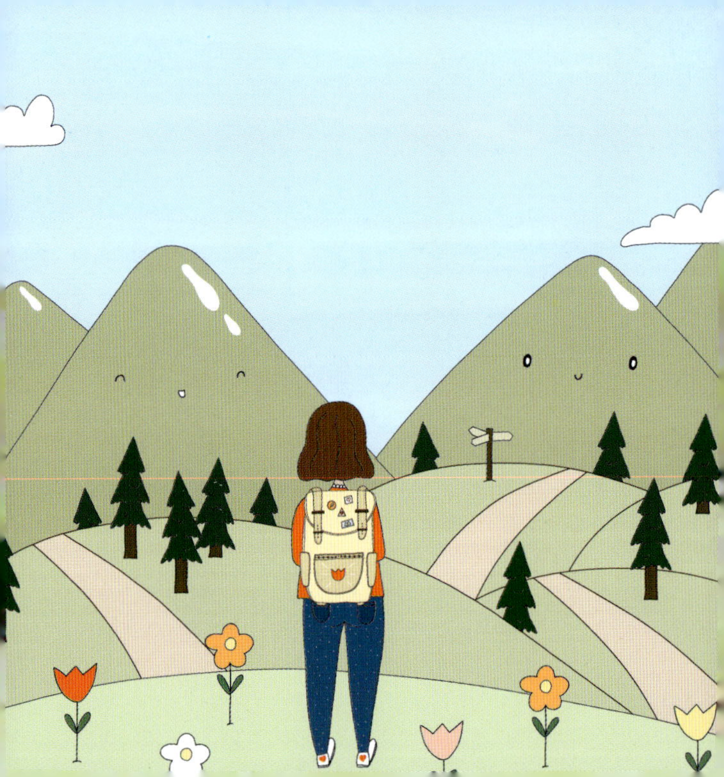

LOOK HOW FAR you've come.

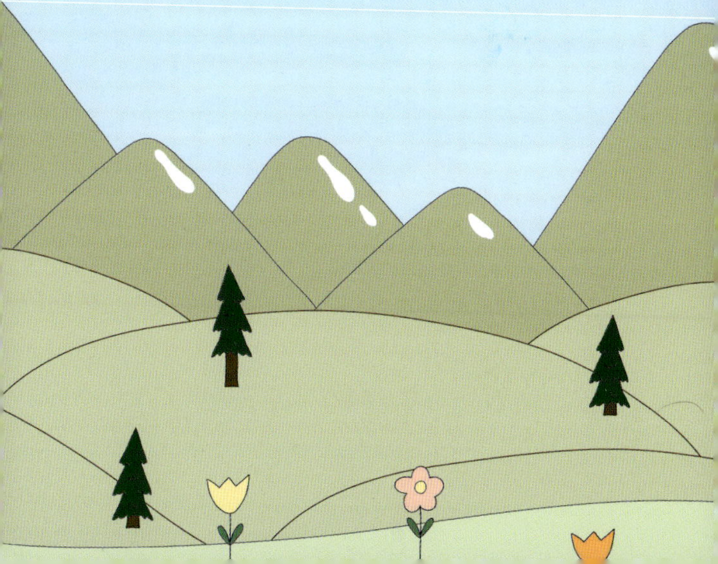

ACKNOWLEDGMENTS

I remember the moment I received the email from Ashley at Familius about this book. I honestly thought they must have the wrong person! I want to thank Christopher & the wonderful team at Familius for your believing in my art & your dedication to creating this book.

A special thank you goes to my editor, Laurie. Your attention to detail, gentle advice, & grammar have made this book what it is today.

This book wouldn't have been possible without my beautiful community on Instagram. Your encouragement & support means I get to do what I love.

Now a big thank you to my family & friends — I cherish & appreciate you. To mum & dad, thank you for your generosity & guidance, and to Tom for your support & love. Kate, thank you for answering my messages about illustrations, & for being my cheerleader & proofreader.

Finally to Sam & Harry, you are my world. Sam, that day you bought me a pencil & sketchbook led to this book. I'm so grateful for your steadfast support, laughter, & belief in me. To Harry, you are my greatest joy & inspiration, & show me every day how to look for wonder. Thank you for encouraging me with your words: "Mama, I like your drawing." This book is for you, kiddo.

Jana xx

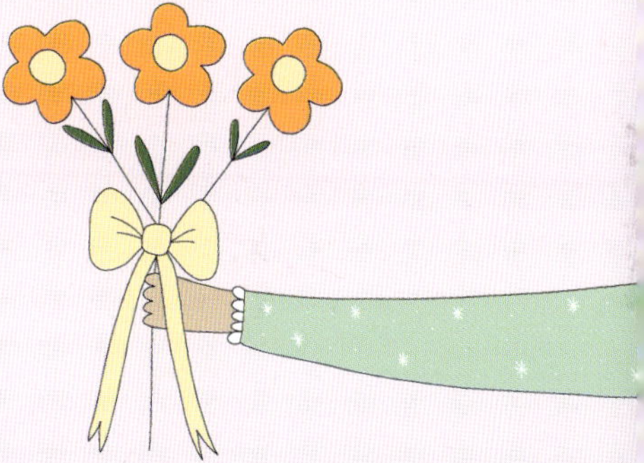

ABOUT THE AUTHOR

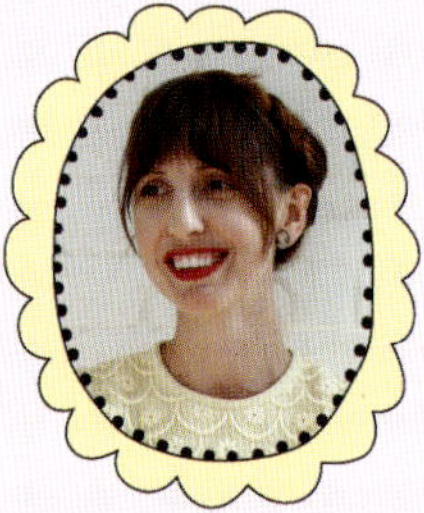

Jana Rushforth is an illustrator & writer based in South Australia. When she became a new mama, Jana decided she wanted to share her uplifting & joyful illustrations with the world by creating @wordfindersclub on Instagram. Most days you'll find Jana drawing & drinking tea in her art deco cottage, where she lives with her husband, son, & growing family of houseplants.

About Familius

Visit Our Website: www.familius.com

Familius is a global trade publishing company that publishes books & other content to help families be happy. We believe that the family is the fundamental unit of society & that happy families are the foundation of a happy life. We recognize that every family looks different, & we passionately believe in helping all families find greater joy. To that end, we publish books for children & adults that invite families to live the Familius Ten Habits of Happy Families: love together, play together, learn together, work together, talk together, heal together, read together, eat together, give together & laugh together. Founded in 2012, Familius is located in Sanger, California.

Connect

Facebook: www.facebook.com/familiustalk
Twitter: @familiustalk, @paterfamilius1
Pinterest: www.pinterest.com/familius
Instagram: @familiustalk

FAMILIUS

"The most important work you ever do will be within the walls of your own home."

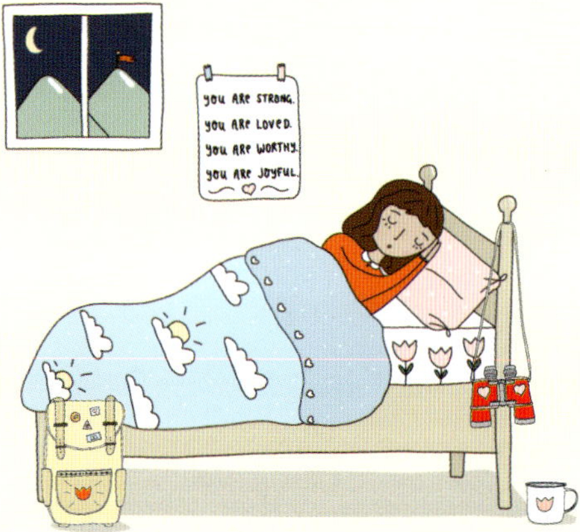
you are strong.
you are loved.
you are worthy.
you are joyful.

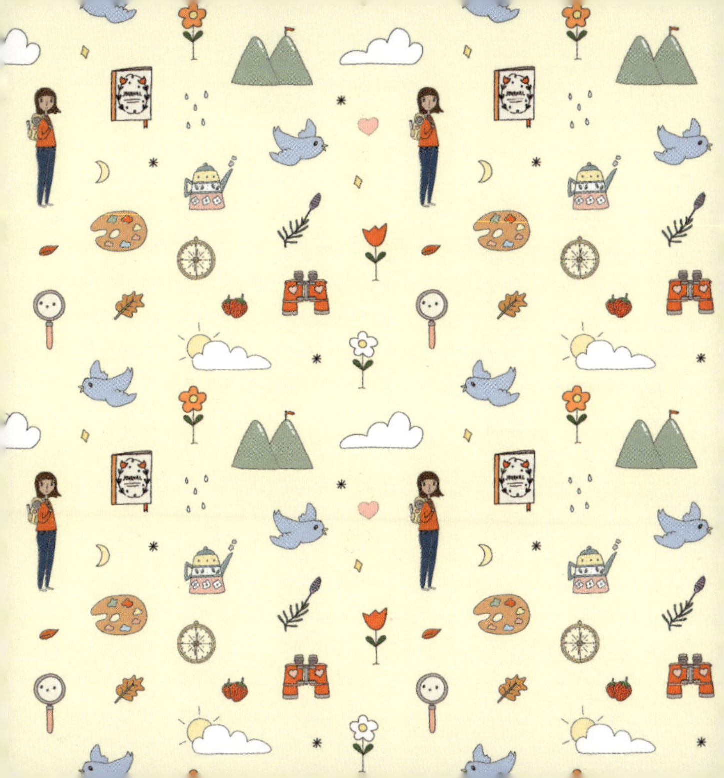

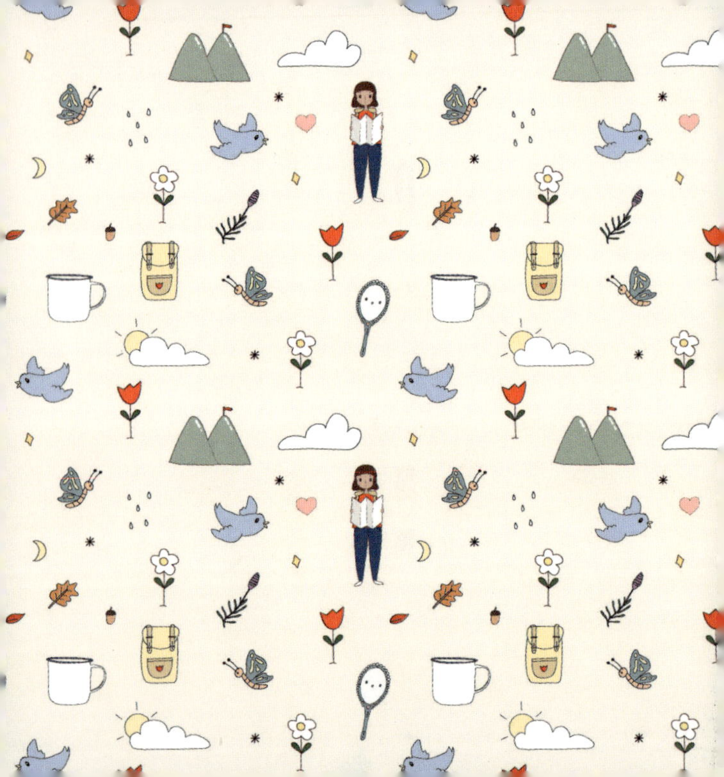